All Tied Up

When I was in high school at Rock Hill High School I could not play football. Having asthma prohibited me from playing the sports that I wanted so badly to play. I volunteered to be the manager of the football team.

That's the guy who tapes up player's ankles and takes water out to the players during time outs. Generally he just assists the players as they prepare for the games and during the games he provides first aid, encouragement and with refreshment. I loved being a manager. I even attended a manager school at the University of South Carolina for a weekend so I could be a better manager.

My junior year our football team was very strong. There is nothing like the team spirit that a football team shares. All the players become one large family and the coach becomes the Daddy. We had such a great spirit that year I wanted to find some way to unite us and to pull together the spirit during a game.

So on the bus as we traveled to that week's game, I took a long white shoestring. I took it around to each player and asked them to tie a knot in it. Player after player, knot after knot was formed. When they were through, it was a short shoestring that was knots from one end to the other. Then I took it to the quarterback, Dennis Partlow. Dennis was one of my heroes and today he still is.

I encouraged Dennis as the quarterback to wear this on his belt as a symbol to the whole team that everybody is pulling together and we are in this knot together. Well, it really inspired the team and started a tradition that week after week game after game they would say, "Where is Ernie with the knot string?" I then made my way to every player letting them tie their own knot in the string that the quarterback would wear and lead us to another win that week.

I will never forget that year as that team pulled together symbolized by the knot. Maybe this is an idea that we should follow today. When we go to church we all could take time to tie a knot in a long rope or in our businesses we take time to tie knots in a long shoestring. Perhaps in a family once a year, maybe on mother's birthday or Mother or Father's day or during Christmas we could take time to tie our knots as a family into a string that is then hung on the Christmas tree each year, just an idea.

Life doesn't have to tie us in.

A Light in the Darkness

INSIGHTS OF A CHRISTIAN SOUTHERN GENTLEMAN

C. ERNIE NIVENS

Inspiring Voices®

A Service of **Guideposts**

Copyright © 2012 C. Ernie Nivens

All rights reserved. No part of this book may be used or reproduced by any means, graphic, electronic, or mechanical, including photocopying, recording, taping or by any information storage retrieval system without the written permission of the publisher except in the case of brief quotations embodied in critical articles and reviews.

Inspiring Voices books may be ordered through booksellers or by contacting:

Inspiring Voices
1663 Liberty Drive
Bloomington, IN 47403
www.inspiringvoices.com
1-(866) 697-5313

Because of the dynamic nature of the Internet, any web addresses or links contained in this book may have changed since publication and may no longer be valid. The views expressed in this work are solely those of the author and do not necessarily reflect the views of the publisher, and the publisher hereby disclaims any responsibility for them.

Any people depicted in stock imagery provided by Thinkstock are models, and such images are being used for illustrative purposes only.

Certain stock imagery © Thinkstock.

ISBN: 978-1-4624-0090-4 (sc)
ISBN: 978-1-4624-0089-8 (e)

Library of Congress Control Number: 2012935061

Printed in the United States of America

Inspiring Voices rev. date: 08/10/2012

I dedicate this book to my "girls":
Rosemarie,
Cathy,
Noelle,
Emily

When I was unconscious and in the valley of the shadow of death, they pulled me through with their constant love and prayers.

ACKNOWLEDGEMENTS

I have to first acknowledge my wife, Rosemarie and daughter, Noelle who tirelessly typed and edited this manuscript. I cannot thank them enough.

I recognize Dr. Alan Walker, who is in the glorious church above, Dr. George E. Morris and Eddie Fox who schooled me in the majestic theology of evangelism of John Wesley.

I offer my tribute to my United Methodist ministerial team: Rev. George Freeman, Dr. Jim Westmoreland, Rev. Angela Burris, and Rev. C.B. Barr. Their frequent appearances in my hospital room enabled me to see the face of God in each of them.

I also have to recognize my business family: Warren Budd, Newnan Georgia, who is probably my cousin and is a great Patriot; Bill Humbarger, Indianola, Mississippi my Presbyterian brother; Jim Erben, Austin, Texas (who successfully defeated cancer this past year), Scott McGuire, Shreveport, Louisiana, who is a constant cheerleader for me; Rosie Franklin, Charlotte, NC who was a great prayer warrior during my accident time; and Thomas Herlong, Johnston, South Carolina, whose merging of faith and work create quite an example. I salute Wes Morris, Kingsport, Tennessee and Boyd Phillips of Marion, North Carolina who I have mentored for a number of years and are my two cheerful sons.

I appreciate and recognize Titus Greene, my client who has become like an older brother to me. His effervescent joy is a contagion to all who know him.

I owe my appreciation to Mark Skillestad, Gastonia, North Carolina, my client and good friend who sat with me countless hours this past year in my hospital room. His joy, willing ear and presence helped me fill many otherwise lonely hours.

Most importantly I thank my Great God who has enabled me to regain my health, cognitive creativity and physical strength. Therefore I am able to complete this dream of mine.

Foreword

I value the privilege and opportunity of commending these unique stories, events and "word pictures" from the life and ministry of my brother in Christ, C. Ernie Nivens. The reader will discover that these writings "light up" and "open up" wide tracts of the Bible to all of us who sometimes find ourselves treading only the well-trodden paths. Here we have the fruit of a very great deal of labor. That the labor was joyfully done is crystal clear. These pages literally breathe energy, excitement and hope.

Ernie invites us to get in touch with the intended meanings of the biblical text and pursue those meaning not only through the experiences of the biblical writers, but also through our own everyday experiences. His love for God's Word is very evident. His readiness for his convictions, shaped by many years of experience, to be reshaped is challenging. His humility is genuine. He has brought the acute mind of a good pastor and businessman into dialogue with Holy Scriptures. We have here much more than a faithful Christian's "work notes." We have A LIGHT IN THE DARKNESS! Again and again, we are reminded that the "mind of Christ" will mark the people of God, only as lives committed to God's world are also committed to God's Word.

Dr. George E. Morris
Senior Professor of World Mission and Evangelism
The World Methodist Council

Aprons

I don't think many of our kids today know what an apron is.

The principal use of my Grandmother's apron was to protect the dress underneath, but along with that, it served as a potholder for removing hot pans from the oven.

It was wonderful for drying children's tears, and on occasion was even used for cleaning out dirty ears.

From the chicken coop, the apron was used for carrying eggs, fussy chicks, and sometimes half-hatched eggs to be finished in the warming oven.

When company came, those aprons were ideal hiding places for shy kids.

And when the weather was cold, grandma wrapped it around her arms.

Those big old aprons wiped many a perspiring brow, bent over the hot wood stove.

Chips and kindling wood were brought into the kitchen in that apron.

From the garden, it carried all sorts of vegetables. After the peas had been shelled, it carried out the hulls.

In the fall, the apron was used to bring in apples that had fallen from the trees.

When unexpected company drove up the road, it was surprising how much furniture that old apron could dust in a matter of seconds.

When dinner was ready, Grandmother walked out onto the porch, waved her apron, and the men knew it was time to come in from the fields to dinner.

It will be a long time before someone invents something that will replace that "old-time apron" that served so many purposes.

Grandmother used to set her hot baked apple pies on the window sill to cool. Her granddaughters set theirs on the window sill to thaw.

Southern style Christianity echoes from generation to generation. It is faith based on the core of the Gospel. In the following pages we will discover and re-discover what Southern style Christianity is all about. Read on.

Applying the Presence

One of the joys of my past life when I was a parish minister for 20 years was serving as a Church Consultant with Churches around the country and even internationally. I remember going to one Church and the whole time I was there people kept saying to me, "You need to go meet Suzie. Before you leave town make sure you have seen Suzie."

After hearing so much about Suzie I couldn't wait. Finally the local minister road me one afternoon out to see Suzie. He told me on the way out that she was handicapped and was bedridden 24 hours a day.

Her brother was an electronics wizard. He had wired the house where she lived. I was amazed when we went up on the porch, rang the doorbell, and this voice came out of this box above the doorbell that said "hello". Then she said "Hey, preacher, both of you come on in." The minister kind of pointed up and I thought he was talking about God for a moment. I looked up and saw the camera that was over our heads.

We walked down the hallway and then took a right into the bedroom where Suzie was. She was sitting up in a hospital type bed. She had no legs and no arms. My heart was stricken with empathy for her. After chatting for a few minutes, she invited me to come closer to her and stand beside where she was in the bed.

She learned that I was to preach that evening at her Church and she asked me what I was going to preach. I explained in a few minutes what my topic was and the gist of what I was going to say that evening. She said, "Oh that's great."

She told me to come closer. In front of her there was placed on the bed a slanted board that had her bible open on it. Beside it was a little shelf and pencil. She leaned over with her mouth, she grabbed the pencil with the eraser pointed toward the bible and she started flipping pages with her head. She would turn to verse after verse where she had underlined the verses and talked to me about how much the verses meant to her.

After hearing eight verses or so I stopped her and I said "Suzie, help me understand. Beside these verses you have written two letters beside each of them, a T and a P. May I ask you what that means?" She put the pencil down and just laughed. She said "Oh yes Ernie, T, P, I'll be glad to tell you."

She said, "Every one of these verses I have applied to my life. I have found that they have been <u>tried</u> and <u>proven</u>, <u>tried and proven</u>, that's the way my faith is with God. With me God has been tried and proven."

I hope one day He can say that Suzie had been tried and found proven. I've got to tell you that I left that day a better man than the one who went there.

I've thought many times about Suzie and her tried and proven method. I would encourage us today that as we live this life with its mountains and valleys to always remember that God's faith and God's presence with us has already been tried and proven. It's only left to us to apply his presence.

Be a Rainbow for Someone

One of the highlights of our vacation in New York was our visit to Niagara Falls. On our first night there we stood by the American Falls and felt the pulsating power cascading around us. Our next day plans included the ride on the "Maid of the Mist" boat to the foot of the Horseshoe Falls.

After getting into our places on the boat, we put on our protective rain gear. The boat headed straight for the base of the majestic falls. The closer we got the slower we moved. Water was showering all about us and we couldn't hear each other over the tumultuous thunder.

Suddenly we broke through the curtain into a place of peace. Behind us the water rolled from above and the sides. Ahead the falls were so close we sensed we could reach out for a touch. There was a sense of peace which must be like being in the eye of a hurricane.

Looking up, beautifully arched over our heads, was a rainbow. The wonder of it all filled our eyes with tears. I held my breath and listened closely for I knew that at any moment some great choir would break out in Handel's "Hallelujah Chorus." There was peace in the midst of the storm!

Isn't that a powerful parable of spiritual reality? So many times we are caught in the thunder and power of life's perplexities so that when it seems we can't bear much more...peace breaks in upon us.

It is difficult to see rainbows from the backside of the cloud. We are encouraged simply to press on, trusting the Rainbow-Maker. The Rainbow Maker never fails!

Storms pass, thunder rolls over the horizon and rainbows await... promises come true. When the rainbow appears, it "hosannas" back and forth across the gray-black sky.

Dear friend, trust God! If you are caught in the thunder, stand in the assurance that a rainbow is coming your way. In the meantime, be a rainbow for someone else.

Be Careful Who You Follow

There's a wonderful story that comes from the White House when Calvin Coolidge was President. He invited some mid-Western farmers to supper in the East Dining Room. They were quite insecure about social graces so they decided to follow the President's lead. When he ordered soup, they ordered soup. He took a soup spoon; they counted off and got the right spoon. He ordered fish; they ordered fish, and so on.

After dinner he ordered hot tea; they didn't like hot tea but ordered it anyway. He put sugar in his, so did they. He poured cream; they added cream. He poured some in a saucer. They looked at each other then repeated. Then the President put his saucer down for the cat!

The mistake of our age is to follow human idols: stage, screen, singers, sports, etc. Just because a certain celebrity drinks Pepsi is not a sufficient reason for us to do so! We are all stained with sin. "All have sinned and fallen short of the glory of God."

Each week it seems that some prominent nationally known figure is repenting on our TV screen. We wag our heads and wonder what "the world is coming to." The world "is coming to" what it <u>always</u> has. The history of humankind from the Garden of Eden to present has been a series of episodes of people trying to be their own god. That includes us.

It is time for us to look that fact squarely in the eye. Sin is not lying, cheating and murdering. We, humans, lie, cheat and murder because we are sinners. We need God's forgiveness, grace, and strength that come through faith and following Jesus Christ.

Indeed, let's be careful not to follow other people! Christ is the only One <u>worthy</u> to follow. Now is a time to challenge our <u>focus</u>.

Be Who You Are

In growing up in Rock Hill, South Carolina, I had a cousin who lived up the street from me. I knew him as "Junior". Everyone in our family called him "Junior". He was mentally challenged but could always be seen riding his bicycle all around town. He had lost most of his teeth, but every time he saw me in the yard, he would stop and give me a big smile. We would talk and laugh. I thought the world of "Junior".

My heart was broken when I learned that throughout the town, he was not known by "Junior" or called "Junior" but rather somebody had given him the nickname of "Acorn". It hurt my feelings horribly to think of my favorite cousin by the name of "Acorn". I refused to call him that.

He was always "Junior" to me. I think there's an important lesson there for us that we should not let the world decide who we are, but to be who we are, not some name of an oak tree seed, but the creation that God has made and placed here in this world.

As my Daddy used to say to me, "Remember your last name. Be who you are."

Be Careful What You Believe

I heard some years ago about a man who worked in a railroad yard in Virginia. It is said that his particular job was to make sure at the end of the day that each refrigerated boxcar's doors were closed. Then no cold air from the refrigeration units would be wasted. At the end of one day, he was closing the doors. One boxcar's door was jammed, and he could not get it closed. So he got up in the car and worked with the door until he freed the jam. The door slammed shut. Unfortunately he could not get out.

He was locked in the boxcar all night long. His family worried when he didn't come home. His coworkers, thinking he had already left, went to their homes. They found him the next morning in that boxcar. He was dead. This refrigerated car would normally have sustained a temperature of about 32 to 38 degrees, but its refrigeration unit was broken. The worker didn't know that.

They found him on the wooden floor of the car with messages scratched into the floor's surface. The first message said, "I am freezing to death." "Tell my family I love them; I am dying," was the second message. And then, he died. The temperature that night never got colder than 53 degrees outside and 55 degrees inside the car.

He thought he was freezing to death, and convinced of that fact in his mind, he froze to death.

Now here is the point of this story. What happens <u>to</u> us is not as important as what happens <u>in</u> us. In our world there are a number of challenges. Sometimes we are rejected. Sometimes we give a lot of time and concern trying to help someone only to have them shut it down with no results. That's the life of a caring Christian.

Not everyone wants to hear Good News. We have to keep remembering that every event has some teaching measure to it. We have to remember what happened to this man in the Virginia railroad yard; his lesson applies. Indeed, what happens <u>to</u> us is not as important as what happens <u>in</u> us.

Burn Away the Sludge

I love being Southern! Our life and culture is full of celebrations, large and small. Having lived around South Carolina, I have gotten to do some amazing things: flounder gigging, cooking (and eating) chicken bog, shrimping with a cast net, tracking deer, fishing for red breast bream, flying an airplane over Table Rock mountain, hanging tobacco, digging Puerto Rican sweet potatoes, and the list goes on.

When there is a nip in the air I think of Guy McCullough. For three years I "helped" Guy make home-made molasses. That means that I kinda hung around and followed his instructions. There's a real art to "cooking 'lasses."

Good molasses come as a result of carefully processed stages. The cane sorghum juice is delicately strained. The juice is poured, a little at a time, into a cooker that is a 6' by 10' copper box over a low red-hot pit. The box allows the juice to flow right to left and then left to right. The juice is held in four separate areas and cooked before being allowed to flow further through the box.

As it cooks, sludge boils to the top. My main job was to take a window-screen dipper and lift the sludge off the cooking sorghum. It takes about an hour for the portioned juice to "cook" from entry to exit. When it flows out the exit hole, it is a beautiful walnut brown.

You can dip your finger under the hot, sticky substance for a taste. You have to close your eyes and set your taste buds for the flavorful explosions of your senses. After finishing we'd go up to the kitchen where we'd sit with fresh vegetables, country ham and sop our plates with biscuits and fresh molasses! Yes, I love being Southern!

What's the point to all this, you ask? Well, isn't it amazing how life's trials can burn away the sludge in our hearts to produce a beautiful faith? Be not afraid of the heat nor the trials – with God we can persevere and be champions!

Deafened By the Circumstances of Life

God is the God of the 'last word.' In our Affirmation of Faith we end it by saying, "I believe in everlasting life." God always has the last word.

In the winter of '86 I was preaching in upper Ohio adjacent to the Maumee River. In a harried-scheduled day, I had two hours available in the afternoon. Bundled like the Michelin-man I took a walk. I had to pause on the bridge over that beautiful river. My face stung from the mixture of the sleet and snow. There were no sounds of traffic or factories. All that could be heard was the river...the whisper of the river.

That river has been there for centuries. Above it has been rain, snow, and blazing heat. It mostly freezes over each winter. People have crossed over, through, and down it. Yet the river continues. I stood entranced by the whisper of that river.

That is how the will of God is. In our lives there are times when we are frozen over. There are times of blazing heat, tornadoes, hail, rain, and thunderous lightning. Still, deep in our hearts there is that constant moving of the whisper of the river of God's will in love and grace. NOTHING CAN STOP IT! NOTHING!

Some of you have been deafened by the circumstances of life so that you cannot hear that whisper in your heart. It is there! The love and presence of God is there giving you hope and courage!

Trust the whisper and let it move within you. In faith pray, "O God, give me guidance for this day. I do not ask for a month, or a week, but for this day." Then pause and listen to God's spirit move within you.

We have Not Been Robbed

There is an anonymous story about an Oriental king who had a particular love for flowers. One day he called in his gardener, handed him a beautiful lily plant, and said, "I wish you would take this into the garden, plant it, water it, and care for it as though it were your very own. I want you to love it as I love it." The gardener was very pleased to accept this responsibility from the king.

The months passed until one day the gardener noted that the plant was ready to bloom again. Early the next morning he went into the garden with great anticipation of seeing the plant in full beauty. To his great disappointment the plant was gone. A feeling of tragedy came over him. He felt robbed.

One of his aides told him that the king had come into the garden and had discovered the favorite lily plant in full bloom. Having discovered this, he dug it up himself, potted it, and took it into the palace.

The disappointment in the gardener's heart disappeared. He realized he had not been robbed at all. The plant had not really been his own. It had only been entrusted to his care and nurture; yet all the while it belonged to the king.

This is the attitude we who believe in Christ must have as we live from day to day. When our loved ones walk the road to death we know that we have not been robbed, for they have been received by the King to whom they really belong.

He has taken them to the eternal palaces and we can but say "Thank You" for the privilege that was ours, for a while, of caring for them and of loving them.

Bury the Hatchet

When we lived near the coast some years ago, we stayed away from the beach in the summer. Our favorite time to walk on the beach was the period from late fall to spring. It was great fun feeding the sea gulls popcorn. They would fly in front of us and eat from our hands as we talked to them.

One day, we noticed some folk working busily near a pier. With hatchets they were chopping some coral and catching crab for supper. They were being so destructive.

Off to the side was a crusty, weather-beaten old man. He carried a bucket and a stick. The stick had a loop of wire on the end. He would insert the stick into a crab hole and pull out a crab every time. While the others were desperately trying to "hatchet-catch" some supper, this wizened man gently and quietly withdrew his supper and left.

Before he left I asked about his secret. He said that the crab is a stubborn crustacean. It will grab hold of the wire on the stick and <u>not</u> let go. He simply would pull them out, break off the pinchers, and set them free to return to their hole to grow some more pinchers.

There is a subtle joy that comes from following the guidance of God's Spirit. Some people live with a hatchet in their hand: feeling that they have to grunt and grind the gusto from life. Noisily they "manufacture" experiences that should be fun but in reality fail to live up to their expectations. The Christian life produces a peace and joy that <u>issue forth</u> from faithfulness.

By My Side

My Daddy fought in WWII in the Alps of Italy near Switzerland. He came home in 1946. My brother, Jimmy was born in 1943 just after Daddy left for service in the Army. Daddy missed the first three years with him.

He was determined to make up with his "war baby"...me. My earliest memory is of sitting on his knee while he fed me at Grandmother's. We were always very close but especially so in the late 60's and early 70's after he had accepted Jesus Christ anew as his Lord and Savior. He used to come "watch" me preach. It made me so proud to have him, Mother and my little brother, Sandy come and be with us.

In 1974 at the age of 50 he was stricken with a fatal heart attack. His death rocked my world! After his funeral I returned home and dwelled in a deep depression for 100 days.

One morning, sitting in dark solitude, I heard a little girl singing "Jesus loves me, this I know." Like the prodigal son, I came to myself and claimed the presence of Jesus anew. I prayed, "Jesus, there is so much I don't know and understand. What I know is that I will place my hand in Yours and trust You." The next song I heard was "By My Side" from the musical Godspell:

> Then I'll take your hand, finally glad
> That you are here
> By my side

It fills my heart to share with you that Jesus has let me walk with Him and my hand is still in His. In my heart I want everyone to know Jesus as Lord to experience the strength that comes from being by His side!

Break It Some More

Gordon Thompson was a great preaching professor at Candler School of Theology, Emory University, Atlanta, GA. He taught us you can say whatever you want, wander around a little bit, and do whatever in the body of the sermon, as long as you finish strong.

I was serving as a Church Growth Consultant for some churches in Ohio and there met Rev. Claude Chivington, from the former Evangelical United Brethren tradition. We got to talking about church conflicts and church "fights"!!

Claude said he once was serving a church so very contentious. One Sunday when it came time for the sermon, he lit an entire pack of firecrackers and threw them into the aisle! He said people went to screaming, running and crying.

When things settled down he told them, "That's what you are doing to this church...you're blowing it apart. Now get to this altar and pray for forgiveness and God's direction!" Everyone came forward and they had an extended prayer time at the altar!

He said that moment marked the turning point in that church's history. They quit fighting and fussing, and started praying more.

Today that church is alive and well because, I am convinced, Rev. Chivington had to blow it apart first!!

So much for "if it ain't broken, don't break it!" Maybe it should be if "it's broken, then break it some more!!!"

The Constancy of Change

There is something about aging that forces reflection. As I stop and look back down the road, I realize that there are not many constants. Of course, the power and presence of God has been constant though my understanding of His nature has shifted and grown. The love of my beautiful family has been constant.

Strange as it may seem, change has been a stabilizing constant. Each day, week, and month has brought its own quantity of change: sometimes with surprise and joy; other times, with sadness and anxiety. Change has been constant!

In my first appointment in 1970, like all South Carolina ministers I was asked to interpret the administrative merging of the black and white conferences. I tried to do so as a good "soldier." After one Sunday's heated debate, Mr. Hamer Smith of Clio, SC extended me an invitation that was rarely given to anyone: to fish with him in his pond.

After a couple of hours of quiet fishing in his invitation only pond, he said, "Ernie, I want to teach you something that I learned at Clemson College in 1917. I had a noted professor who taught me how to 'cook frogs.'" He had my attention!

He continued, "If you heat a pot of water to boiling and throw in the frog, he'll jump out. The change is too quick and life-threatening. But if you'll put that 'ol frog in a pot of cold water, let 'em swim a bit, you can turn up the heat a little bit at a time and you'll cook him!"

"Ernie, change is like that. You're doing the best you can with a difficult situation. Keep going!"

"Mr. Hamer" didn't realize how much he helped me. He is in heaven now. "Mr. Hamer", I thank you!

Change is like that. It is constant. Your world, like mine, changes each day. If we look at that change in the perspective of time and distance, we can cope and be happy at the same time. God bless you and let's keep going! "Mr. Hamer" symbolized Southern style Christianity for me!!

The Christian Rhythm

Not long ago I went with three cars of youth and adults to a Methodist Camp, Asbury Hills, at the base of Caesar's Head Mountain in South Carolina. We hiked five miles of rough terrain on an old logging trail. Heat and humidity were high. We talked, laughed and shared to encourage each other.

Half-way around the trail, known as the "Loop," we crossed one of many trickles of water across the trail. I had learned years ago that this trickle leads to a majestic waterfall.

We followed the trickle to a rock-bed creek then around a deep descent. Suddenly there opened before us a free falling waterfall that cascaded onto some rocks.

We went prepared for this moment. We were steamy hot from the rugged climb up the mountain. We stepped into the pool of water to discover that it was (seemingly) ice cold!

After our bodies adjusted to the temperature change we screamed with joyful delight. I stood under the waterfall letting its chilly fingers massage my aching back. I drank from its pure sparkling cold fountain.

The exhilaration of the experience is indescribable. Refreshed, we made our way back down the Loop to our cars and then to home. We slept well Sunday night!

To me this is a parable of how worship should bless our lives. After a week of laboring in the "world", we come to Sunday School and worship met by the refreshing water of God's presence in song, prayer, sermon, and sharing.

Then refreshed, we journey back to our "worlds" of work, school, and community fully alive to share God's love and help build His Kingdom!

This is the rhythm of the church: gathering to study and worship together then out into the world in service in Jesus' name.

Daddy's Live in Us

Isn't ice wonderful? Year round I really enjoy iced tea, soft drinks, and especially water. Many Seniors have memories of the Ice Man driving his delivery wagon, placing blocks of ice in the ice boxes in homes. I collect miniature ice wagons. So far I have found two and keep them on a shelf in my office. There is a reason.

My Grandmother told me a childhood story about my Daddy, Cecil Nivens. As a boy he was quite mischievous. Grandmother said that during hot summer days, she often would remove her false teeth while working around the house. More than once she would look out the door and see my Daddy run behind the ice wagon, jump up on it, and get a free chunk of melting ice.

She would dash to the door and yell as best she could, "The-thil! The-thil! Get off that i-th-e wagon!" (You have to say it out loud to make it work!) My Daddy died in 1974 so I collect ice wagons as a way of staying in touch. I like ice year round!

Father's Day is an important day. We salute the honor and the memory of Fathers, Dads, Daddies, and Pops. Jesus taught us much about a Father's love.

My Daddy learned well. I give God thanks for a Daddy who taught me never to quit; who said things like "cain't never could!" and "you won't know until you try!"

Before my first sermon he said, "Ernie, I've never preached but I've had to listen to a lot. The only advice I have for you is two things:

One, remember the word KISS: Keep It Simple, Stupid,

And two, always to preach Christ."

Over twenty years of preaching and almost twenty of teaching Sunday school, I have tried to follow his advice and in the dark times to hear his voice of encouragement. Thank you, God, for Fathers and Daddies!

Diving In

As a boy, one of my favorite hobbies was to go swimming in the giant pool at the YMCA in Rock Hill, South Carolina. It was open in the morning from 10 to noon, in the afternoon from 1 to 5:00 and evening 6:00 to 10:00. In the summertime, I lived in that water.

I joined the swimming team even though I had asthma as a child. I learned that my best contribution to the swimming team was in diving. I learned to dive on the low board and the high board and to do flips, swan dives and a one and a half backward flip. They taught me wonderful dives and I thought I was pretty good at it.

I really enjoyed diving off the high dive, especially doing a 1.5 flip until one day I hit the board with my head and put a crack in my skin. I had to go have it stitched up and stay out of the pool for a few days while it healed. Once it healed, I was right back into the pool going off the high dive.

One evening when I was preparing to dive off that high dive, I noticed this woman had her little baby. Her daughter was maybe year and a half, two years old. She had her by the hands and she was walking along the edges, dipping the child into the water and pulling her back out: into the water, back out, into the water and back out. She finally got around to where she was under the diving board.

I waited a few minutes until she could go by. This time when she dipped her child into the water, she lost control of her grip. I can still see that little girl struggling in the water as she sank toward the bottom. I immediately dove off the high dive in a swan dive that took me straight to the bottom. I grabbed hold of that baby and bounced off the bottom and pushed her back up out to the air where she coughed and spit up the water and caught her breath.

Then the lifeguard was there in time to lift her up and set her back on the side. Her mother came and hugged me and said, "Thank you for saving my baby." I said, "Please ma'am, don't do that anymore. Get in the water with her, try not to dip her anymore." She said, "Don't worry. I will. I've learned my lesson." I don't know who that little girl was or the mother, but I've had the best joy in my life recalling that moment when I actually saved the life of another human being. I would like to know who she is today, but that's okay because God knows. And God knows I did that.

We have moments in our lives when we encounter people that are drowning in their grief or their fear or their worries. Our call as Christians is to dive in after them, to help them grab hold of their spirits and to move back toward the air, the light and the joy of God's presence. There is a lot of emphasis today on witnessing as Christians. It is nothing more than doing just what I said, diving in where they are and helping them find the fresh air of God's presence, love and grace.

Diving To The Rainbow

The first of January causes me to reflect on a powerful event in my life. Some years ago I was in the Fiji Islands on a preaching-teaching mission team with the World Methodist Council. After being in the "bush country" for two wonderful weeks, we gathered back at our hotel for some "R&R". We chartered a boat for a day of snorkeling in Suva Bay.

On the trip out to the coral reefs the water was murky. An old iron coated tug was awkwardly half submerged. I began to think that this rendezvous was not a good idea. We put on our fins, mask, and snorkeling tube and jumped in.

Suddenly a different world exploded upon my senses. The underwater coral was a rainbow rock. Millions of tiny fish eagerly moved to eat bread from our hands. We would dive deeper and the 80 pound blue fish would ascend to commune with us. It was exhilarating!

What a parable of life. Daily we are content to run our routines, grinding our grooves into ruts. Life can become so "usual." When we hear Christ's challenge to "follow" Him and "take up our cross" suddenly life becomes a living rainbow.

Let us jump deeper into our faith, there to see all the grand and glorious things the Lord has prepared for us. Then let's extend a hand to another with the invitation to "come and see." Lord, help us to have the courage to experience Southern style Christianity.

Evangels of Care

I heard a company CEO recently use the word, "Evangel." I began to think about what an evangel really is. You probably know that it is a "messenger of good news."

Now that doesn't make every reporter on television an evangel. They don't bring good news. They bring mostly sad, sorry, bad news. They are not evangels, but we are.

To understand evangel, we have to look at the historical origin of the word. Here my biblical studies come to bear.

In the Old Testament there is a history of Israel as they made their way out of Egypt and were looking for the Promised Land, a place to settle. After escaping through the Red Sea, they made their way to the desert. I believe that NASCAR is founded on a biblical foundation. Why? Because the Hebrew folk made left turns in the desert for 40 years! Sounds like NASCAR to me.

Moses got to see the Promised Land before his death. Then the Hebrews moved into the Promised Land. Time and time again they encountered people of other cultures and beliefs who disputed their right to do this. Wars resulted.

While all the men went off to battle, the women, children and old, old men stayed home. They were left to wonder day after day what was happening to those they loved.

They, of course, didn't have CNN or text messaging or any of the ways of communication of our age. Instead they had a system. They would look to the mountains and watch for a runner to come over the mountain pass. Once they saw the runner they saw the news.

If the runner was carrying swords and arrows, they knew the war was continuing. It might even be advancing toward them. They had better pack up their goods and get out of town in a hurry to save their families.

If the runner came over the mountain carrying items of greenery, palm and olive branches, that was a symbol to those who could see him that they were in for a time of peace. Whenever they saw the runner bearing the green branches, they broke into celebration, singing, laughing, dancing and feasting.

These were happy days for the land of Israel. They rejoiced because they and their children could settle there and enjoy their lives together in a time of peace and, hopefully, prosperity.

The Greek name for that runner coming over the mountains is *euangellion* (pronounced, *ewe ahn gel e ahn*).

Today it's the same thing. People are watching for the runners, the people who are bringing to them good news, messages of hope.

I hold out to you, my friends, that we Christians are this generation's Evangels. We are Evangels for Care for we bring great good news of hope, grace, forgiveness, joy and life eternal that people may use to help them have a life of love, peace and hope. We are Evangels for Care.

Friend of the Witness

A friend of our family tells me that while studying at the seminary at Emory University, she was involved in an auto accident in Atlanta. A man ran a red light and plowed into her, demolishing her car. The investigating officer determined that there were no injuries or witnesses and reported so on the official accident report. He also said that he would assess no blame but let the Judge do so in court.

Our friend says the other driver came to court in a neck brace and on crutches. He was accompanied by another man. The Judge listened to both stories. The other driver's friend spoke up and told a third version. The Judge asked whether he had witnessed the accident to which he mumbled and stammered. The Judge asked again with more conviction and he confessed that indeed he had not seen the accident but he was a "friend of the witness" who had. This infuriated the Judge and the case was naturally ruled in our friend's favor.

Upon hearing this story I howled! I realized how so many of us are "friends of the witness." We fail to be witnesses to Christ and like Peter "stand afar distance." When it comes to our faith we are not determined to be a witness but safely affirm that we are a "friend of the witness."

It was that kind of insincerity and lukewarmness that crucified Jesus! That level of commitment is dangerous both for the believer and for the building of the Kingdom of Christ.

May God give us the courage to move from being a "friend of the witness" to being the real thing!

From Pain to Joy

*O*n July 1, 2007, I had the wonderful opportunity of taking our dog, Maggie, for a run. I had trained Maggie, a beautiful Australian cattle dog, to strike out on her own. I would follow behind her on a bicycle. She was not on a leash. She was just free to run, and I would give her a voice command. She would turn it up and run with such fervor and excitement in front of me. I would fly on the bicycle behind her.

At 10:15 p.m. on that night, several deer ran in front of us. We had nowhere to go. I must have tried to avert hitting the deer, lost control of the bicycle and fallen over backwards. We were riding on an asphalt driveway in our subdivision. I cracked my head in the back.

I don't remember that or anything for the next month. All of July holds no memories for me. The next thing that is clear is July 28 when I had been home with my wife for an entire day.

Rosemarie and our girls tell me so many things about my experiences in that month. I almost died. They operated at 5:00 a.m. on July 2 because I had a "subdural hematoma" and my brain was swelling. The surgeon, with his great skill, saved both my life and my cognitive abilities. In the days to follow, my "four girls" stood by my bedside caring, praying and crying for me. I knew nothing of their being there. Now that I know these things, my heart is so filled with the realization of how committed they were to the husband and father I am. They tell me that I "woke up" about ten days after the accident.

I would greet visitors by name, talk to them and give Rosemarie and our daughter Noelle instructions about following up on cases, but I have no memory of such things. The mind is a wonderful thing to protect us from the pain that it is experiencing while still letting us "be ourselves".

The next events of my life that I actually was fully aware of came a day after I got home from the hospital, July 28th. August and September were clearer still.

I am so thankful to our loving God who chose to leave me here so I could continue in this wonderful mission of being an Evangel of Care.

I am so blessed to have a family who gathered around me and loved me until I was well. Then there was my second family of fellow workers and clients who gathered around me and my family with such wonderful care.

There are no lasting problems from that accident. I am fully cognitive and recovered, but I, also, realize that God left me here for a purpose.

There are more people to receive our care. There are more chances to share God's love, grace, peace, forgiveness, and joy. We are called to help them in our role as an Evangel for Care. Are you ready?

The Future Isn't What It Used To Be

The future isn't what it used to be. Fifty to seventy five years ago it was popular to say that the modern world had discovered practically everything that could be discovered. A Boston newspaper carried this item: "Joshua Coppersmith has been arrested for trying to extort funds from ignorant and superstitious people by a device which he says will convey the human voice over wires. He calls the instrument a telephone." Indeed, how ridiculous!

Around the turn of the century H. G. Wells predicted with detail such futuristic things as the "automatic dishwasher" and the "electric cook stove." Lee Deforest, one of the great pioneers of radio, made a prediction that was printed in the New York Times in 1926. He said, "While theoretically and technically television may be feasible, commercially and financially I consider it an impossibility, a development of which we need waste little time dreaming."

Our age consistently asks, "Is there any hope? Is there any good news for these days?" The answer is "Yes, there is!" The future is in God's hands. As a favorite hymn says,

> "This is my Father's world.
> O, let me ne'er forget,
> That though the wrong be oft so strong,
> God is the Ruler yet."

The future belongs to God! It is His gift to us. By faith the future is placed into our hands.

He has given us the freedom to do with it as we will. Let us seek to do all in our power to invest ourselves for a better tomorrow. That task is done one day, even one hour, at a time. The future isn't what it used to be...it can be even grander.

The Game Is Not Over Yet

It was New Year's Day in the 1930 Rose Bowl. Roy Reigels of Southern California picked up a Georgia Tech fumble, but began to run in the wrong direction toward his own goal line. One of Reigels' own teammates finally tackled him, but Tech took the ball and scored right before half-time.

Reigels cried like a baby in the locker room. Coach Price quietly said, "The same men who played the first half will start the second." The team trudged out--all but Roy.

"Coach, I can't do it. I've ruined you. I've ruined Southern Call. I can't face the crowd."

The coach touched Reigels' shoulder and said, "Get up and go back. The game is not over yet!"

Reigels went back and Tech players say they never saw anyone play football like Reigels did in the second half.

Perhaps some of you are discouraged or confused about the direction your life went over the past year. Perhaps as you look back you see some areas where you ran the wrong way.

God is the opportunity God. A review of the Old and New Testaments will demonstrate person after person who ran the wrong way and through faith in an ever-present God, got up and ran in a new direction!

Our faith says, "Get up and go on! The game is not over yet!"

Getting Scorched In the Rear

I like Election Day! We have heard many pleas to encourage us to vote. We know that America is a truly blessed nation with the possibility of liberty and justice for all. Voting is a direct act of freedom…a freedom that has been bought with the lives of many Americans.

In December 1983 I stood at the Demilitarized Zone that separates North and South Korea. I had worshipped with the South Koreans as they prayed for the reunification of their country. They have family and friends in the Communist North that they have not seen since before 1953.

I stood at "Freedom Bridge." There was nothing about that bridge that represents freedom. Soldiers and citizens, even U. S. soldiers, have unlawfully darted across it never to be heard from again. After visiting the DMZ, I returned home a more grateful American.

It was decades ago, during much the same kind of critical election years we face, that Abraham Lincoln made his earthy comment on responsibility at the polls: "It is the people's business. The election is in their hands. If they turn their backs to the fire and get scorched in the rear, they'll find they have got to sit on the blister."

I don't know about you…but next election, I am going to vote. Too many God-loving people have given too much for me not to vote.

We are indebted and responsible to them. See you at the poll!

Getting Tuned Up

Along time ago a letter was sent to the National Broadcasting Company ("NBC") from a prospector in the hills of Montana. Written on a piece of paper from a brown bag stuffed into an envelope was an unusual request. "I am a regular listener to your radio programs, and as a friend, I want to ask you for a favor. It gets lonely up here, and besides my radio and my dog I have not much else for company. I do have a violin that I used to play, but now it is badly out of tune, would you be kind enough at seven o'clock next Sunday night to strike me an "A" so I can put that fiddle back in tune?"

At first the officials smiled at that request. But then the manager of NBC thought about it, and the request took on a bit more perspective. So the following Sunday night the network interrupted its scheduled programming to sound an "A" and give their friend his pitch.

Well, sometimes we get out of tune. At those times we need to get the "pitch" again. In fact, it's not a bad idea to start out each day by getting the pitch from God. The notes will be on love, forgiveness, patience, kindness, wisdom, etc. This kind of getting in tune is called prayer.

An American clergyman, Ralph Cushman, wrote:

"I met God in the morning
      When my day was at its best,
And His presence came like sunrise,
      Like a glory in my breast...

So I think I know the secret,
      Learned from many a troubled way,
You must seek Him in the morning
      If you want him through the day."

So if you are not in tune today...why not go to God right now and have Him strike an "A" for you. It will be done. Then face the rest of the day confidently knowing He is with you!

Heavenly Dusters

One of the first churches I served was a beautiful place built in the financial heydays about 1913. Unfortunately the flu epidemic killed so many thriving business men. The membership of this church was devastated as well.

Still the remaining few took great pride in the beauty as well they should. One lady in particular, Fayne Hamer would come every Saturday with her dusters.

The church had a sectioned choir loft with a brass rail across the front. Mrs. Fayne was insistent that that brass be cleaned and not be allowed to tarnish.

Saturday after Saturday she polished that brass rail. On Sunday morning it would sparkle under the sanctuary lights.

I give thanks for all the Mrs. Fayne who love to do God's work diligently behind the scenes to enable others to worship in joy and pride. Surely our church has some people like this whom I call "Heavenly Dusters."

With each of us doing what we can, then our churches shall remain centers of spiritual strength and infectious places for the growth of the family of God through Jesus Christ.

I am confident that today Mrs. Fayne is polishing the golden streets of heaven!

Handmade Evangelism

For several years now I have noticed those big scripture signs at significant sporting events: Super Bowl, Monday Night Football & Baseball, Golf tournaments, Olympics, Indy 500, etc. In bold letters we read "JOHN 3:16", "II COR. 5:17", "ROM. 5:8". They pop up on bed sheets hanging from the upper decks, behind home plate, over the golfer's head as they putt, and posters beside the runway at the Miss America Pageant.

I have wondered what organization was coordinating this consistent-persistent display. Well, it is not an organization but Rockin' Rollen Stewart; his wife Margaret; and a friend, William King. They have a modest life-style in a Toyota van, driving 55,000 miles per year and speaking to any religious group that will invite them.

They receive love offerings in order to buy tickets from scalpers. Then with a hand-held television, get in line with the right camera angle. Rollen said in <u>People</u> magazine, "We are evangelists who want to get everyone to read the Book and we reach millions."

You see, Rollen Stewart knew a time when he was addicted to alcohol and drugs. They had him by the throat choking the life out of him. His life fell apart!

One Sunday morning he was watching a church worship service on TV. "I saw immediately how I could take the Word of God to the world," he said. "I fell to my knees and allowed Jesus to take control of my life." Since then he has been spreading the Gospel, free of commercial cost, through every TV camera he can.

I confess I find it a bit irritating to see him waving back and forth when I'm caught up in a good ball-game on TV but I salute his eagerness! He is right. He is an evangelist. Evangelism is simply spreading the Good News any way we can. We leave the results to God.

We may be annoyed by ever-present Rockin' Rollen but there are people who have discovered New Life by his persistence. I like his way of "doing it" better than many people's way of "not doing it!" God bless you, Rollen Stewart.

Heaven Will Be A Great Place

Growing up in Rock Hill, South Carolina, I was a member of two large families. Family reunions were always so much fun. My father was one of eight children which meant lots of cousins. Reunions were held regularly. I enjoyed seeing all my cousins. I have many memories of my Moon cousins. My Daddy also had eight brothers and sisters, thus many cousins. My mother' maiden name was Moon. My father, of course, was a Nivens. So, I guess you could say that I'm a "half-moon" and my children are "quarter moons".

I remember with great fondness the memory of every Christmas going across the street to my Aunt Hazel's house where all of my mother's family would come, her brothers and sisters and their children. Aunt Hazel lived in a four room millhouse, much like our house. Believe it or not, we got 50 to 60 people in this house on Christmas morning.

Uncle Ernest would hand out the presents that surrounded a giant tree in the living room. The presents went halfway up and around the tree. Uncle Ernest would play Santa Claus and call out the names of each of us to receive presents as we had given each other gifts. You held all your presents without unwrapping them and then when all the gifts had been given out, every family would break away in different parts of the house. I think some of us went outside, where we'd open our presents and take delight.

We would open them one by one and enjoy seeing what each person got. I remember one year my daddy gave my mother one of those hairdryers that you sit in a chair and pull this big cone down over your head to dry your hair. Everybody in the family, all 60 aunts, uncles and cousins, had to come by and take their turn sitting under this new invention of this magical hairdryer. My mother was overjoyed to have such a tool to help her be so beautiful.

That's a foretaste to me of what heaven will be like where all of us will gather and share each other's love, joy and tell the stories of our lives. We'll appreciate how God helped us in so many ways while we're here.

It will be like Christmas morning at Aunt Hazel's with lots of loudness, laughter, joyfulness, and singing. I look forward to the great reunion there. Heaven will be a great place, but I can wait a little bit longer before I go there.

Hoboes in the Night

When I was a little boy growing up on the Mill Hill in Rock Hill, South Carolina on summer nights I used to stay out and play with my friends until it was dark. Our house was near a railroad track that was mounted on a large mound of dirt. It probably was 100 feet tall as it went through our little community. The trains would race through there making such rackets morning, noon and night.

It was commonly known that there were hobo's that traveled on those trains and sometimes when the train was backed up it would stop on top of that hill and we could see hoboes jumping off the train to camp in the woods on the other side of the railroad track. Sometimes we'd go over there during the daytime.

We could see where they camped and they left little cans of Sterno where they camped. They cooked out for a while before catching the next train and moving on. Sometimes they'd stay in the woods for several days before traveling.

Whenever I stayed out to play late at night I could hear my mother and my daddy calling me to come home. It would be pitch dark. I would run for a couple of blocks through the darkness going home. A couple of times I'd have to travel over what we called the "back alley" where the trash truck came to gather trash.

When I ran over those alleys I was so scared there might be a hobo hiding there waiting to rob me or harm me. So all the way home I had learned as a boy to recite a scripture, Romans 8:31. It is the scripture that says "If God is for us, who can be against us."

I would shout that over and over and over, repeating it all the way home, "If God is for us who can be against us." That gave courage to my heart to know that I was going to be fine until I could get home; if God before us." Let us remember that word in these days.

If You Play With Fire

On a particular Monday I walked into the county jail to see Billy (name changed.) He had carried his uncle to see a man, a fight erupted, and the uncle murdered the man. The uncle then forced Billy to drive him away. Billy was arrested as an accessory to murder.

He was in his darkened jail cell. I felt like I was at a zoo seeing some reluctant animal move from the comforting darkness to the austere light near the bars. We talked through the bars; their coldness symbolic of the distance between a warm spring day and the darkened solitude of the cell.

I reminded Billy of God's love and grace. We talked of hope for a chance at a new life. Before I left I gave him my pocket cross as a reminder that Jesus knew the fear and darkness of prison. We talked about how Jesus turned a terrible situation of horror into an avenue of possibility of forgiveness for millions throughout the ages.

Upon leaving the jail, when I walked back into the sunlit, warm day I had to stop on the steps. There were pink azaleas by the walkway that had escaped my attention on the way in. The air was clean, sky blue, and birds melodic. The contrast of the past half-hour overwhelmed me.

"Dear Lord, help Billy (and all the other Billys) to know that with You all things are possible. Enable us to rejoice in the rebirth of the earth. Motivate us to share Your love with others so that Billy's situation might not be repeated. Move us to be champions of love, justice, hope and grace. Give us courage to be your witnesses in these demanding days. For Jesus' sake. Amen."

I Have a Dream

Rosemarie and I have seen Momma Mia on Broadway twice and the movie once (so far). It is a beautiful story of Sophie trying to find her birth father before her wedding. The story is developed by weaving in the music of a group called, "ABBA".

It is such a delightful experience that in the New York productions people would actually dance in the aisles and at their seats. It is an infectious experience.

How I wish that our worship services could engender that response within us. We should approach the worship experience with a sense of expectation ready to see what God will unfold within us as individuals and as a group of believers.

The concluding song of Momma Mia is a heart-felt soliloquy by Sophie as she adores a full moon and sings:

"I have a dream, a song to sing
To help me cope with anything
If you see the wonder of a fairy tale
You can take the future even if you fail
I believe in angels
Something good in everything I see
I believe in angels
When I know the time is right for me
I'll cross the stream - I have a dream."

As Evangels of Care this could be our theme song.

I Have a Great Opportunity For You

I like words. I like to search for meaning behind words and their derivation. Our English word, "opportunity," comes from the Latin "op" which means "toward" or "facing" or "entrance" or "access." "Portune" comes from "Portus" which means "harbor" or "port." The word goes back to ancient sailing times.

You see a little sailing ship caught in a storm. The wind howls and the waves break over the deck. Terror grips the hearts of the sailors. Day after day, night after night, they are driven by the storm (Acts 27). Through the darkness and the fog, land is sighted, but the coastline is rugged with jagged rocks.

Then they see it!--A protected harbor where they will be safe. When they see the entrance to that harbor and decide to sail toward it, they eventually enter it. That is the meaning of the word "opportunity."

Opportunity is when you are no longer lost in the storm. The recognition of opportunity has deeper significance than we usually imagine. The word originally dealt with the critical issue of survival itself.

It has been so trivialized and cheapened today that many of us are suspicious of the word. If someone says to you, "I have the fantastic opportunity for you to get rich quick..." I hope you will keep walking!

In Jesus Christ we have undiscovered opportunity! Perhaps right now you feel caught in a terrible storm--this way and that. Perhaps the coastline seems totally rock-bound.

The word "opportunity"--"oportus"--announces the existence of the entrance to the safe and fulfilling port. History is replete with people who have found "opportus" in Jesus Christ. Also Jesus has discovered in many people an "opportunity" to reach through them to receptive, seeking people.

He sees individuals who are searching desperately for a harbor, a home, a place of belonging, an "opportunity." He calls us to a new focus! He invites us to help Him! He says, "Share your time, your talents, your resources-- with me; don't hold back. I need your help."

Our response is the key to opening the door to the unlimited, undiscovered opportunities. As we together discover the entrance to the harbor--let's reach out to share this Good News with other boats! We have great opportunity!

Immortal Diamond

Westminster Abbey in London is a majestic center for worship. It also is a burial ground for royalty and holds monuments to great people who have impacted the history of Great Britain and the world. In a remote part of the Abbey is the "Poet's Corner" where significant poets have engraved marble floor monuments. I stood above the one for Gerard Manley Hopkins. Beneath his name are two words, "Immortal Diamond."

"Immortal Diamond" is a poem in which Hopkins witnesses to the power of God through Christ to transform his life. It reads:

> "I am all at once what Christ is, since
> He is what I am, and
> this Jack, joke, poor potsherd, patch matchwood
> is
> Immortal Diamond."

Hopkins is saying that before Christ he was a common person: "Jack", no one took him seriously, "joke", worth as much as a broken earthenware pot: "potsherd", and no more purpose as the cheapest wood in making matchsticks: "patch matchwood." But by faith in Christ, he was transformed and empowered with purpose and mission, so much so, that God made him an
"Immortal Diamond."

Can there be a greater epitaph than that? In the corner of Westminster Abbey this silent witness trumpets the majestic faith that is ours through Christ.

I don't know about you but that brings tears to my eyes and a burn to my spirit! If you are unhappy with your life, my friend, Christ can touch you and make you an
IMMORTAL DIAMOND.

Is This The Place?

My wife Rosemarie and I have been married at the time of this writing for 41 years. We met in the nursery of the church we both grew up in. We were both babies at the same time. There's only ten months difference between our ages. When she turned 14, I all of a sudden looked at her and thought, "Wow, who is that?" We began to spend time together and date.

I knew even then I would marry her one day. I told my best friend then when I got older I was going to marry her. Well our relationship during high school was off and on a couple of times but since high school we've been together. We got married when we were both barely out of high school and have grown up together. We've had a wonderful family with three daughters, and we all grew up together.

I was a United Methodist minister for 20 years. Rosemarie was the ordained minister for 15 years. We have moved from here to there, in each place trying to find a sense of "home". I remember one time we moved to a new appointment and we stayed the first night at the Holiday Inn. We were in the pool in the summer time and Emily asked me, "Daddy, is this our home now?"

I told her, "Emily, our home is wherever our family is together. Yes, the Holiday Inn is our home for tonight. Tomorrow night we will be in a new parsonage." That has been our way – with Rosemarie and me - for 41 years.

One of our favorite songs throughout all these years has been the song, "Somewhere." "Somewhere there's a place for us." It comes from the musical "West Side Story."

When we were in parish ministry, we couldn't afford to buy a house. But now that I've been retired from parish ministry for 20 years and have worked as a financial planner for those 20 years, we own our own house.

Rosemarie ordered that line from that song, "Somewhere there's a place for us." It is a wall adornment. I stood on our sink in the kitchen and mounted the beautifully scripted phrase on the wall "Somewhere there's a place for us."

This house became our "somewhere." If we were going to name our house, it would be called "Somewhere." Yet we have known for a long time that a house is not our place. Rosemarie wrote a sermon one time that was influenced by a preaching professor named Fred Craddock. She adapted a sermon of his that says that God is the place.

I can report in this writing that for both of us, God has always been the place for us on the mountain tops or in the valleys. Even over the last year with our health challenges, we have found God anew to be the place for us. Where is your place? I hope and pray that you will discover, if you don't already know, that God is the place for you.

The biblical reference goes back to Abraham and Sarah as they were moving – every time they would settle, God would have them move again – move and move and move. Sarah would ask Abraham, "Where is the place? Where is our home? Where is the place?"

Abraham wouldn't know how to answer that and then finally Abraham asked God, "God, are you the place?" And God said, "Congratulations Abraham, you've asked the right question. Yes, I am the place." For all of us who call ourselves Christians, who have come to know the love of Jesus Christ in our hearts – for us, the heavenly Father is the place – the place where we live – the place where we hope – the place where we dream. Thanks be to God for being our place.

A Letter to My Daughters

Dear Cathy, Noelle & Emily,

So now it is the year 2000. I remember in the fourth grade, my teacher Mrs. Ashe talked one day about the year 2000. At that point in my life, it seemed an infinity away. There is much about life I don't understand and can't explain but I have learned a lot since the fourth grade. Most of the important things in life you are going to have to learn first-hand. There is no real training manual entitled, "Coping and Succeeding in the New Millennium."

Life is like the military description of "OJT – On the Job Training." You learn things as you go, look back, wish you had done things differently, then make adjustments for the future. Your Mom and I tried early in your lives to instill basic qualities and values of life. Those attributes, of course, became quite fuzzy during your teenage years though they came into focus once you rounded the curve of 20.

It is not in my power to give you what I would like for you to have in this new century. I can remind you of a few things and point you to others.

➤ I would remind you to have a dream. Without a dream for your life, each day becomes a rut like yesterday. Ruts grow in depth until they become a grave. Dreams keep you on your toes – vital and fresh for the opportunity of a new day. I remember my Daddy saying, "Ernie, shoot for the moon, if you hit the street light at least you got off the ground."

⅄ I would remind you that failure is never final. Walking is conditional falling. It is only the next step that keeps us from going face down. There are times when we do fall. I have discovered that happy people are the ones who stand up the fastest. Here is the key: when you fall, pick up something. Learn from the experience so you don't have to fall over the same stump twice.

⅄ Learn to trust people. People will step on your heart on a regular basis. I have learned it is better to trust and be hurt than distrust and grow cynical. Just try to keep the same person from stepping on your heart twice.

⅄ Your family is like the sunshine of a new day. Friends come and go – co-workers change – neighbors move away. The one constant relationship is your family. Protect that relationship at all cost. Where else will you be able to run for strength, encouragement, and comfort, but to those who know you best and love you most.

⅄ You have heard me say this thousands of times –"Remember who you are." Life and friends will try to mold you into the conformity of comfort and familiarity. You were created unique. Be who you are –stay unique – and remember you last name.

⅄ One of the things you tease me about is when I tell you to "Take a picture and lock it away in your heart." What I try to do is encourage you to seize the moment. Life tries to get us to focus only on the future. By doing so we miss many of the simple experiences and pleasures of the present.

⅄ Each day is filled with little moments that are too valuable to run past. When one of those moments breaks in on your hectic pace, make your feet stop, open your eyes and all your senses and grab it! Enjoy it for the present moment and then tuck it in your heart. In life's dark days it is the accumulation of those little moments that echo light into that present darkness.

⅄ Remember that you are created – not manufactured. There is a God who ordained you with personality traits, hope, love and faith. It is that living God that remains the one and only constant in a life of consistent changes.

⅄ At the bottom of every dark abyss is the rock of God's presence. If you are in that abyss, discover the rock and push off, back up toward light and the fresh air of faith. God will not fail you, nor ever leave you alone.

Of course there is much more I could share with you- not to worry-I will.

Walk boldly into the new millennium...you are loved.

Daddy

A Letter To Noelle In The 5th Month Of Pregnancy

Dear Noelle,

Hold your son! Every hour of your life from now until June is an opportunity for you to hold your son with an intimacy that will never be duplicated the rest of your life.

From the moment he is born, he will pass into the hands and lives of many people.

♥ The medical team will take him for his first moment in preparation of living.

♥ You will hand your son over to his father for the very first time.

♥ Not long after, you will hand him over to those who provide daycare in your absence.

♥ You will hand him over to school where day by day and year after year various teachers will hold his mind and heart in their hands.

♥ You will hand him over to his friends, both at school and community.

♥ You will have to trust his actions and relationships beyond your oversight.

♥ You will hand him over to a girl and then another girl and another girl until the day comes that you sit in the front pew and watch him give his heart to his bride.

♥ He will give his heart to the business world and every now and then remember to check on Mom.

I do not mean for you to despair over all this giving. I just want to encourage you to seize the power and joy of these days as you hold your son all to yourself. Then, as an infant, to hold him tightly and whisper "motherly" secrets in his ear.

His squirming you alone now feel, his heartbeat is tied to yours, and through the tube of life you provide his breath. Cherish these months of your life, for their memory will support you in the coming days of separation. He is God's gift to you so cherish each moment and event. God trusts you.

This is the Blessed Joy and Trial of Solitude called Motherhood.

A Light in the Darkness

School bells will be ringing again! So will alarm clocks and ears. Families will be readjusting schedules as swimming pools are being exchanged for car pools.

Many of the influential people in my life have been teachers. In many cases they became extended parents and short-term members of our families. When I think back over my school days, there are some teachers who emerge from memory...

Miss Ligon--my "single" first grade teacher with whom I fell in love, but alas she married another;

Mrs. Glenn--2nd grade, who looked stern and sounded "mean" but had gentle ways of encouragement;

Mrs. Ashe--5th grade, who was so patient, loving and soft spoken until one day she threw the eraser at "Snake" Davis;

Mr. Hugh Williams--Northside School math whom I see occasionally, (It wasn't me who put that potato up his car's exhaust pipe!);

Mr. Perry Aycock, my elementary school principal who had a wide paddle, a great smile, and wore a tie every day.

Mrs. Lucy Goode, high school English and speech, who pushed me to develop my speaking skills and helped me win a few oratory contest metals;

Ms. Catherine Moore—high school chorus teacher who enabled me to fall in love with music by introducing me to Rodgers and

Hammerstein. She also deepened my faith by teaching us a very reverent singing style of "When I Survey The Wondrous Cross". We sang it during a stormy morning assembly session. During the last chorus, demands my soul, my life, my all" the sun broke through the clouds and flooded the auditorium with a majestic, brilliant warmth.

Miss I. Ruth Martin—who, in college, got me excited about studying the Bible;

Dr. Beverly Blackmon--English professor at Francis Marion College, who helped me hear messages beneath symbols. Her enthusiastic support of my impersonation of Mark Twain I will never forget.

Dr. George E. Morris—Candler School of Theology seminary, who helped spark a passion for mission and evangelism and open national and international doors for study and preaching. He enabled me to discover John Wesley's theology of evangelism.

The list can include many others! In essence, I give thanks for those faithful teachers who invested themselves in me. We have a good many friends who are teachers and involved in education. As they begin each new year, pause and breathe a prayer for them. What they do is of critical importance. Pray that they may follow the example of the Great Teacher, Jesus Christ...and be a Light in the Darkness!

Let Your 'Yes' Be 'Yes' and Your 'No' be 'No'

Each time I served as a Missioner by the Board of Discipleship in Nashville, my heart was rekindled. One particular New Life Mission in Spencer, Iowa was a fantastic event. The Church has spent much time in study, prayer, and preparation. I consulted, taught and preached in 24 settings in 5 days. It was exhaustively exhilarating.

On Tuesday, Pastor Dick Pearson and his wife, Remalee took me on a beautiful tour of the Iowa Great Lakes, particularly East and West Okoboji. These are magnificent blue water lakes that are filled to the brim. Various species of migrating birds were evident. They also told me about the University of Okoboji!

On Thursday I was inducted into the Booster Club of the University of Okoboji (U of O) and presented an official sweatshirt, cap, window decal, and tickets to the annual football game between the U of O and the winner of the Iowa/Iowa State game. It will be played on Saturday, September 31st at Our Lady of the Lakes Stadium. I have 12 tickets for Row A, Seat 1 on the 50 yard line.

Before you get too excited and charter a bus, I need to tell you that the U of O is fictitious. It's all a part of a local gag created by a men's clothing store, "The Three Sons." In addition to selling very fine clothes, they sell thousands of dollars in various U of O shirts, caps, cups, etc. To really "fit in", one must have their official University of Okoboji gear!

It was a lot of fun and you may see me in some of my U of O gear. The point of all this is to remind us not to make our church membership vows like the diplomas from the University of Okoboji.

Let's not just talk a good game, but may our commitment of time, talent, gifts and service be for real. As Paul said, "Let your 'Yes' be 'Yes', and your 'No' be 'No'".

Let Your Light Shine

I was serving a church in a different city from where I lived some years ago. This church sat off of a main thoroughfare highway. Hundreds of cars passed in front of it daily.

When December came, we had a grand plan at this church to erect a roadside giant style Advent Wreath. As you know an Advent Wreath is a green wreath with candles sticking in it, three colors, two that are purple, one pink and then one in the middle that is white.

I got the men's club of the church to help as we constructed this giant Advent Wreath. We got chicken wire and rolled it into a large wreath and then we stuffed pine branches in it to make it a verdant green. We made candles out of stove pipe that were 6 feet tall. The white candle in the middle was a 6.5 foot candle taller than the rest. We had an electrician wire them so we put some lights in the top of them to look like the fire on top of the candle. It was absolutely beautiful.

Each week that passed toward Christmas we would light an additional candle but the white candle in the middle is not lit until Christmas Day.

One day I was in the office at the church and Mrs. Grace came by to see me. Mrs. Grace's husband had died earlier that year and she was having a tough time adjusting to his absence.

She told me "Ernie, I've got to tell you something that happened to me yesterday. I had been home and I was riding back to town to pick up a few things from the store. I drove in front of our church and I looked over at the giant Advent Wreath.

The lights were lit and in the middle of the Advent wreath there was a blond haired teenage girl wearing all white. She had her hands clasped above her head and she was standing like a life size candle inside this Advent wreath. She lifted my burden and gave me such peace and hope as

I looked at her joy. I don't know who she was but I wanted to tell you in case you might know who she was."

It didn't take me but just a second to say, "I know exactly who it was. Her name is Lori." I asked her "Would you mind if I thank Lori for you." She said "Oh please do. Tell her she made a tremendous difference in one old woman's life by doing what she did."

I approached Lori and thanked her for what she did and told her what she had done to bless the heart of Mrs. Grace. Lori cried, moved to know that she had made a difference in somebody's life by doing something so simple.

Now this is a symbolic story for us, and it calls us to realize that we don't have to stand in football stadiums with a great big sign reading "be saved now" or read John 3:16. No, we only have to offer our love in God's grace and peace to those who are near us.

We all have a mission around us, whether it's at school or work or shopping or even at church. We're not all called to stand in the pulpit and preach or sing solos or pray aloud while everyone is silent.

We're simply called like Lori to let our light so shine that others will see God's love shining through us. That's what we're called to do as Evangels of Care.

Listen To the Music

My brother Sandy was a master in music by playing an organ and singing. Before his death in 1995 he played the organ for a Catholic Church in Columbia, South Carolina. He would go every Saturday late in the afternoon to practice for about two hours for Sunday's Mass.

Most of the time when he first started practicing he was in the Church by himself and then the last two years of his life he said that there was an old man that would come in and sit on the back row of the Church and listen to him as he practiced. This went on Saturday after Saturday after Saturday. After some length of time Sandy's curiosity got the best of him.

He stopped one Saturday and walked to the back of the Church, introduced himself to the old man. He told the old man how moved he was that he would come every week to listen to the organ as he practiced for the next day. The old man then said that he looked forward to every Saturday because it was the highlight of his week and he would not miss it for anything. He then told my brother Sandy his name. Believe it or not it was Frank McGuire.

If you don't know who Frank McGuire was he was born in New York City of an Irish American family. McGuire was a basketball coach in the NBA for a while but is renowned for coaching college basketball. He holds the record for the most victories in a season without a loss; together with Bobby Knight of the 1976 Indiana Hoosiers. His record was 32 and 0. What a record.

He achieved the number one ranking of the best basketball team in the U.S. with two universities... The University of North Carolina Tar Heels and the University of South Carolina Gamecocks. He was elected to the Basketball Hall of Fame in 1977. McGuire is well loved by the players who played for him and all of us who watched him coach at our favorite colleges; in my case University of South Carolina Gamecocks.

When Sandy found out it was Frank McGuire who was coming Saturday after Saturday to listen to him he was absolutely blown away because Sandy was an industrial strength Gamecock fan. He and Frank developed quite a relationship in the final days of both their lives. Frank McGuire died November 11th, 1994 and my brother died less than one year later.

I'm glad now that they are together in the heavenly music hall listening to indescribable music as they sit on the same pew together and smile at each other in their enjoyment.

Love Now

We salute our Senior Citizens every day. As the "Baby Boomers" of the U. S. grow older we are developing a new appreciation and affirmation for our elders. It is about time. Other countries have rich traditions of looking upon the aged ones with honor and respect.

Last week I was leaving a "retirement home after visiting. There was a beautiful sight in the front yard. An elderly woman and what appeared to be her granddaughter were visiting and <u>working</u>. The Grandmother, sitting in a rocking chair in a flower bed, was bending over pulling weeds and planting seeds. The granddaughter, taking instructions was dutifully assisting with hoe in hand. They were laughing and chatting, I sat in my car, a joyful spectator of this picture of life's fullness.

Two thoughts came to me. One was a reminder that it is important to demonstrate our care. It is not enough to have deep emotional, even sentimental, feelings if we do not give expression to them.

This granddaughter had taken her Grandmother from her room, out of the building and into the garden.

Secondly, it is important to take time to express that care <u>now</u>. Mac Davis sang a tune to remind us to "stop and smell the roses." I think of a little ditty I heard some time ago.

> Bring me all my flowers, please, today;
> Be they pink, or white, or red;
> I would rather have one blossom now
> Than a truckload when I'm dead."

Loving Father??

If you drive up Highway 17 north of Myrtle Beach you will pass a long stretch of wooded land on the right. The only thing of notice is a large roadside mailbox labeled "Baba." North Myrtle Beach, South Carolina houses the center of an international cult, "The Lovers of Meher Baba." Meher Baba means "loving father" in Hindustani. Baba was born Merwan S. Irani in 1894 in Poona, India. He proclaimed himself the new incarnation of Jesus Christ. He recruited many wealthy followers thereby establishing orphanages, hospitals, schools, and shelters for the poor.

Baba is most noted for his silence. From 1925 until his death January 31, 1969, he spoke nothing. He wrote volumes and gave lectures with the help of blackboards and alphabet boards. He promised to eventually speak the "One Word" that would bring world peace and spiritualize the world. He set dates to break his silence and postponed each one. He died in an auto accident near Knoxville, Tennessee.

When I visited the Baba Center, I, also, visited in a man's home adjacent to it. This man was going blind and chose to spend his last days painting beautiful portraits of "Baba". He expressed to me his deep conviction that one day Baba would resurrect and that then the world would understand and believe! I came away depressed for that man whose faith was growing as dark as his vision. To date Baba has not resurrected.

The <u>only</u> faith that worships a living Savior is Christianity. As the philosopher Kierkegaard said, "The resurrection stone hangs around every philosopher's neck."

Jesus made and makes true his promise to always be with his disciples and followers. Ask any mature Christian and with confidence as sure as the sunrise you will hear, "I serve a risen Savior!"

There is no mountain so high or valley deep that the risen Christ is not there. There is no problem too great or joy inexpressible that excludes his powerful presence. This is not a theological truism. This is the testimony of my heart! It is tried and proven Southern style Christianity.

Merry Noelle

*O*ur middle daughter is named Noelle. When people hear her name they ask us if she was born at Christmastime. Of course, Noelle means Christmas in French. We just laugh and say, "Oh, well, in a way. She was born July 2nd. She was our Christmas in July, and she always has been our Christmas in July. She's a joyful, wonderful happy young woman now." I have the delight of having her work with me in my business.

I remember many years ago when she was about 12 years old. Her mom and I had been to a meeting several miles away from where we lived and we asked our neighbor to look out for Noelle and her sisters in the afternoon when they came home from school. We pledged to get home as quick as we could. We did so.

You can imagine our fear when we drove up to our house and saw an ambulance sitting in our driveway with all of its lights glowing. Our hearts just fell down, not to our stomach, but they fell down to our big toes. We didn't know what to expect with three daughters inside that house.

We ran in and lo to our eyes, we saw Noelle on a chair in front of the refrigerator. The freezer door was open and her arm was extended into the freezer. Of course, our first question was, "What happened?" We found out that she had stuck her finger in the icemaker because she was curious whether the water coming in to make ice was hot water or cold water.

She thought she would stick her finger up in there and feel it to see the temperature of it. The little arm that knocks the ice out after it is frozen came across the ice receivers, the ice formers, and caught her finger in one of the little holes up there where the water was going to form the ice.

She was caught and couldn't get her finger out and couldn't get the arm to move. She was stuck there. That's why they called the ambulance to come, to see if they could lend a hand to freeing her up. Well, it took them awhile. They had to remove the icemaker from the freezer and then undo the arm and get her finger out of that little contraption that she had caught it in.

Noelle's always been curious about life. That was an extreme moment in her life when she was so curious about the temperature of the water. We still laugh and tease her a little bit about that even today.

She has two boys of her own: Justin and Ryan. We warn her about letting them get near the refrigerator in case that curiosity is a genetically passed concern.

I recall when Noelle was much, much younger. She was only two years old. I was a minister in the Methodist church at that time and we moved to a new church in a new town. It was right after my father, her grandfather, had died.

I had taken that pretty hard myself and had battled some deep depression over his death. He died when he was 50 years old. I was 27.

I'm sure Noelle picked up on my depression that I was battling. As I tried not to withdraw from the family, she'd withdraw a little bit. She wasn't laughing, she wasn't making fun like she usually does. So Rosemarie and I came up with a strategy, that we would just immerse her with hugs all the time.

Whenever we saw her we'd just grab her up and give her a big hug – over and over and over, hug after hug after hug. It didn't take us but about a month to pull her out of wherever she was. Then when she saw us she would run to us for a hug.

She's still like that today. I can't tell you her age, but she's over 30, under 40; but every time I see her it is like something sparks in her where we move to each other with great hugs. When I hug her I see her, again, as the little two-year old, three-year old girl who withdrew from the world and then found her love and joy once again.

Today her joy is abundant and she passes it to everyone that she knows. Family, friends, even people she meets in stores. She is such a joyful young woman and I love her so. She's, also, a very devoted Christian. She helps teach Sunday school. She takes her two boys to church with her husband, Bo. To look at her you can see the love of God in her eyes, and God's presence in the joy of her smile.

I'm so glad that, as her parents, we were led by God's spirit to surround her with hugs for a while. I thank God for his leadership and his guidance in helping us save the emotional life of our wonderful daughter Noelle. Thanks be to God.

More than Adequate

Aprominent businessman ordered a Rolls Royce car and was immensely impressed with it. One day he went to the car dealer and asked him what its horsepower was. The dealer said that the Rolls Royce Company never stated the horsepower of their engines. The businessman specifically asked the dealer to find out.

Because the man was an important customer, the dealer sent a long cable to the Rolls Royce works in Derby, England, setting the exact specifications of the engine, asking them to cable immediately the exact horsepower. Shortly the reply arrived, bearing one word: ADEQUATE!

Some of you have come to know the comforting, "adequate" power of God's Spirit. You have walked through life's dark valleys with a loved one. You have struggled against doubt and despair.

You have experienced almost unbearable physical and mental pain. You have swooned toward the ground only to find strong but unseen Arms lifting you up and helping you to go on.

Some of you have come to the end of your rope with very little strength to carry on and have found God's strength as "adequate" for whatever need you had at the time. As St. Paul writes in Philippians 4:19 "And my God shall supply every need of yours according to His riches in glory in Christ Jesus." "Adequate" is hardly the word for that.

God is able to do far more than we could ever imagine. We're not looking for strength to just "hang on" but to go and overcome!

The wisest man or woman in the world today is the one who can see where God's Spirit is working--who knows where the flow of power is going, and goes with it. Our task is to discover what God is doing in the world and to do it with joy! The strength for the task will be more than "adequate"!

The Need Is Urgent!

One of the joys of 20 years in ministry is to share with people in new and exciting ways. While serving in Newberry, SC, I was invited to be the Chaplain of the Newberry Fire Department. That experience held some joyful, fearful and tearful moments. Some of the firemen were volunteers who risked their life to save others.

I close my eyes and still see four firemen crawling into a burning doorway, dragging a hose, seeking to save the lives trapped inside. I confess to you, I prayed and cried as I anxiously waited for their return. It was powerful!

I wore a monitor so that if needed an alarm would sound and directions would be given to the fire's location. That alarm tone meant that response was needed and urgent! There were no extra minutes for questions--just urgent response!

It occurs to me that our age is sounding many alarms: cries for help from those being engulfed in the smoke and fire of a life without hope. Sometimes the cry is very silent. Often the cry is stated by absence--from work, school, home, and from laughter. The cry is real and it is urgent.

When Jesus walked the earth he talked of the urgency of the Kingdom of God. Two centuries later the urgency remains. John Wesley said that he needed "now" people.

The hungry of the world can't wait for committee action after a tabled motion. Our youth and children can't wait until the week-end. Our neighbors need us before warmer weather and cooking-out days get here.

God needs us! You are needed to teach children, sing in the choir, share your faith with those who love you, give more abundantly to support our missionaries who are laying down their lives in service, and the list goes on...

Please do not wait for someone to give you a personal invitation. The voice of Christ compels us now. The need is urgent! This is the time for response!

Nothing Can Stop It!!

God is the God of the 'last word.' In the Apostles' Creed, we end it by stating, "I believe in everlasting life." God always has the last word.

In 1988 I traveled England with thousands of Methodists from around the world for the occasion of the 250th Anniversary of the Conversion of John Wesley. We journeyed by first class train dining cars to the famous spots of his life: Oxford, Bristol, Gloucester, Birmingham, York, Epworth, and of course London. It was a spiritually exhilarating experience.

The last night in London I found that I could not "let go" for the return home. So I walked the streets of London until the wee hours of the morning. At one point I stood on the Westminster Bridge over the River Thames nearest Parliament.

I had to pause on that bridge over that historic river. There was very little sound of traffic or factories. All that could be heard was the river... the whisper of the river.

That river has been there for centuries. Above it has been rain, snow, and blazing heat. It mostly freezes over each winter. People have crossed over, through, and down it. Armies and navies of various countries have traversed it over time. Yet the river continues. I stood entranced by the whisper of that river.

That is how the will of God is. In our lives there are times when we are frozen over. There are times of blazing heat, tornadoes, hail, rain, and thunderous lightning.

Still, deep in our hearts there is that constant moving of the whisper of the river of God's will in love and grace. NOTHING CAN STOP IT! NOTHING!

Some of you have been deafened by the circumstances of life so that you cannot hear that whisper in your heart. It is there! The love and presence of God is there giving you hope and courage!

Trust the whisper and let it move within you. In faith pray, "O God, give me guidance for this day. I do not ask for a month, or a week, but for this day."

Making Some Corrections And Adjustments

I once had a wonderful experience in Continental, Ohio. I was there as a guest church growth consultant and preacher. The worship services were inspiring, hospitality warm, weather warm then cold: eight degrees, pies delicious, and Christian faith and love enriching. It is powerful to go to a new place and see how much in Christ unites our hearts.

On Wednesday Rev. Stu Huffman, Pastor there, and Rev. Claude Chivington, retired minister, were taking me back to the Fort Wayne Airport. We traveled over beautiful West Ohio farmland. The earth has just been turned its first time preparing for this year's corn and soybean crop.

The roads there are long and straight. One can see for five miles up and down the road. We rode for 12-15 miles without having to stop. Then suddenly we approached a stop sign in open country. The intersecting road had the right of way. Our road continued but it was offset by 8-10 feet at the intersection. Stu informed me that as the roads were being paved years ago one paving team started at the east side of the county and one at the west side. They met at this junction and were off by a few feet from each other. I figured that wasn't too bad considering they were working with primitive surveying tools from so great a distance.

Isn't this a parable of Lent? Lent is a time for self-evaluation. It is a time to check out how "straight" is the road we are traveling. It is a time to make some corrections and adjustments. Let us pray that our Lord will give us courage to see the adjustments needed and then to make them. May we seek to live lives that are "on line" with Jesus' call to take up our cross and to follow Him.

One Shovel At A Time

I once shared in a project that I really enjoyed. A High School basketball coach invited me to be the "Team Chaplain". This role afforded me the opportunity to sit on the bench with the team, share in strategy sessions in the locker room, give a "pre-game" talk (with a little magic), and counsel with some of the players.

It was therapeutic for me to get into the game, scream, clap, and jump around! It's great for stress reduction!

One night the team faced a crucial game. It was a must win! Prior to the game I told the players that sometimes we face seemingly impossible tasks. Jesus' words have always bothered me when he said, "Say to this mountain to move and it shall." I have never been able to "move a whole mountain!"

Then it occurred to me that it is possible to move a mountain--<u>one shovel at a time</u>! We talked about playing one minute (shovel) at a time. They did. The other team never led and our team won--due to great coaching and determined desire.

This principle is as true in our lives. You and I often face the impossible--mountains that loom before us. We <u>can</u> move that mountain: one shovel at time, one day at a time.

Remember Jesus said, "Seek ye first the Kingdom of God and all these things shall be added unto you: (Matt. 6:33). Friend, keep up your chin! Keep digging! The mountain will move!

Offering Your "Thumb" To A Funeral Procession

'll never forget the first time I conducted a funeral in Greenwood, South Carolina. After leaving the Funeral Home, there is a two mile stretch where I was leading the procession to the cemetery. I had an anxious feeling to have a long line of cars following me without police escort. I had never traveled the route before. Thoughts of panic raced through my mind--"What if I miss the cemetery?--Have we gone too far or not far enough?"

As we crested a hill I noticed a male hitchhiker with a small carrying bag. He pleadingly extended his thumb into the lane of traffic as far as possible. He even smiled warmly.

When he recognized that I was leading a funeral procession the thumb recoiled, the carry bag dropped to the ground and his whole body stiffened. His non-verbal language shouted for me to ignore him!

I chuckled and began to think how true to life was this man's plight. How often do we desire something in our hearts only to find out that it really isn't what we wanted after all? How often we are willing to seek "greener grass" without careful thought and preparation. How often we have "thumbed" a funeral procession!

In Jesus' day many people were "thumbing" life: looking for the Messiah, the Deliverer, God's anointed One. How often they followed anyone who gave easy answers to difficult questions. Yet, are we any different today?

The Opra Ain't Over!

The Dallas Cowboys were struggling to stay in the race for the playoffs. On a banner on the forty-yard line of Texas Stadium a devoted fan hung a sign of encouragement:

"THE OPRA AIN'T OVER 'TIL THE FAT LADY SINGS"

It was his way of saying "We're hangin' in there, baby. Don't count us out! We're not givin' up! The opera ain't over!"

Sure is easy to jump to conclusions, isn't it? We are all informed that so-and-so will, <u>for sure</u>, wind up doing such-and-such. At times it's downright scary. And discouraging!

Every once in a while it's helpful to remember times when folks wound up with egg on their faces. Much to our amazement, the incredible often happens.

- Like that time the world didn't end;

- Or Truman beat Dewey;

- And the communists didn't take over America by 1980;

- And Muhammad Ali could get beaten.

Yes, at many a turn we have all been tempted to jump to so-called "obvious" conclusions, only to be surprised by a strange curve being thrown our way. God is good at that. When He does, it really encourages His people.

Can you recall a few biblical examples?

- A wiry teenager, armed with only a sling and a stone, whipped a giant over nine feet tall.

- With an Egyptian army fast approaching and no possible way to escape, all looked dark. Not so! Against nature and reversing the pull of gravity, a sea opened up and allowed the Hebrews to walk across.

- AND THAT DEAD-END STREET AT GOLGOTHA MIRACULOUSLY OPENING BACK UP AT AN EMPTY TOMB THREE DAYS LATER.

You may be reading this while backed up to a set of circumstances that seem to spell T-H-E E-N-D. Your adversary would love for you to assume the worst. He'd enjoy seeing you heave a sigh and resign yourself to depressed feelings that accompany defeat, failure, resentment, and minimum faith. The One who brought His Son back to life takes delight in mixing up the odds as He alters the obvious and bypasses the inevitable.

The blind songwriter, Fanny Crosby, put it another way: "Chords that were broken will vibrate once more." God has a beautiful way of bringing good vibes out of broken chords. When the Lord is in it, anything is possible!

THE OPERA AIN'T OVER!

"Play Ball!!"

Back in the 1980s, I had quite an experience in my life where I borrowed some stationery from a local newspaper and wrote the Atlanta Braves baseball team for a press pass package. They sent it to me.

I went to Atlanta for four days living as a reporter. Each day I would go to the stadium at 3:00 in the afternoon. I had a pass to go into the clubhouse where the players were. I would do so and chat with them. I played cards with them and got to know them as best friends because I was and still am a great Atlanta Braves fan.

When it came time for batting practice, I had a pass that allowed me to go into the field and to talk to them as they took batting practice for both the Braves and the teams they were playing against. I also had a pass that after the game I could go back into the clubhouse and talk to them about the game, joining in the interviews with other reporters about those who had performed well in the game.

For three days it was the most fun a human being could have. I was like an eight year old walking in the room with all my heroes.

Each night they prepared in the press room a large buffet for all the reporters. What great fun it was to mingle with reporters and have the great food that they prepared. On Friday evening, after I had fixed my plate, I turned to find a place to sit. The room was packed. I saw one chair at one table of four. I walked over to it and asked the gentlemen at the table if I could sit there.

One of them whose name is Ernie Johnson, a regular TV announcer for the Braves, said "By all means have a seat. I guess this is the table for us Ernies." He was Ernie, and I was Ernie. I looked up and saw the other two men and was stricken by great surprise.

Across from me was sitting the great Vin Scully who was known by millions from his broadcasting baseball games for years and years. Seated next to him between us was another baseball announcer who was a retired baseball player by the name of Joe Garigiola. I told myself internally, "Ernie shut up and don't say a thing."

That's what I did. I sat and listened to these great baseball stories from these three wonderfully seasoned men. In a little bit Ernie Johnson asked me who I was reporting for, and I told him the name of the newspaper where I was living at that time, although I was just a Methodist minister taking a few days off in reality but I didn't tell him that.

During the game, I took my position in the camera box down on ground level right behind home plate. When I got home they told me that night Ernie Johnson, who was calling the game, made the announcement that "we are glad to have Ernie Nivens here tonight reporting for his newspaper. I had dinner with him and he's quite a nice chap".

When I got home, people teased me mercilessly about becoming a paper reporter for the Braves. It was a fantastic experience to get close and to see what it's like to live as a professional baseball player.

I witnessed there before the game a prayer meeting of some of the players as they knelt in the clubhouse and prayed for each other. They prayed that God would keep them safe during the game, to help them perform their best with the gifts He had given them. I came away from that experience with a renewed love for the game of baseball, especially for the Christians who play baseball and commit themselves to using God's gifts so wonderfully.

The Reality of the Changed Life

While on a mission to the Fiji Islands in the South Pacific, I met a man named Jone Dabea, pronounced "Johnny Domm-be-a". Jone worked as a golf greens keeper for one of the luxury resorts.

One day he found the wallet belonging to an Australian tourist which contained credit cards and over $3800. Jone's annual salary was $300. This wallet contained the equivalent to ten years of Jone's salary. (Multiply your annual income times ten.) He turned the entire wallet into the authorities and would not take a reward.

I found this story difficult to believe so when I preached in Jone's village I asked to meet him. He assured me it was all true. Teasingly, I asked him, "Jone, why didn't you just keep the cash and turn in the wallet?"

He smilingly responded, "The old Jone would have but I'm a new Jone. Jesus has made me new so I am honest!" Jone was talking about the reality of the changed life.

We don't hear very much about this anymore. The reality is that we can be made new by our faith in Christ. If you are grinding your groove into a ridiculous rut, you can be changed. This change happens by faith and following.

The disciples of Jesus caught the attention of their world by being new persons:

John, "Son of Thunder" became the "apostle of love";

fickle "Simon" became "Peter the rock";

"Mary Magdalene", the happiness-seller became the "first proclaimer of Easter".

The story goes on and on...

When lives burn with the passion of Christ:

> churches grow, budgets are exceeded, Sunday School is staffed and filled, choirs sing joyously, sanctuaries are filled, homes become places of peace, jobs and schools become mission centers, somber faces are lit with hope, resentment turns to patience, scowls become hugs, darkness edges to dawning and dawning to noon-day bright.

Sounds rather exciting, doesn't it!

Let us pray that the Church of Jesus Christ is emerging here, there and everywhere!

Rainbows Come After the Storm

Courtenay and Warren Budd are like my sister and brother. Several years ago their son, Bryant was missing two years and three months.. Each day drug by and each night seemed a decade long.

Long searches were conducted yet no clues were discovered. During that time, they went to the beach for some solace and prayer.

Courtenay says she was walking the long beach, praying with heart-felt passion. At One point she prayed, "Lord, please give me some kind of sign that I will make it through this!"

She had been walking toward a dark, gloomy sky and decided to turn around and head for home. It was about a mile of her walking away from the storm. She then noticed a woman she did not know walking straight toward her. The woman said, "You've got to turn around, you're missing it!"

Courtenay turned and saw a most majestic double rainbow. Her eyes filled with tears and in her heart she just knew this was the answer to her plea.

No, the story did not end with music and white doves flying. Bryant was found, dead, although his sprit is now with God.

Hundreds of friends surrounded Courtenay and Warren with love and broken hearts for them. Bryant's fraternity almost filled one half of the church for his funeral.

Yes, rainbows normally appear after the storm has passed. This one occasion I am confident that this wonderful, fear-filled woman needed some kind of blessed assurance.

Thus a rainbow appeared as a reminder that she, and now we are never alone. Our God through Jesus Christ has promised never to leave or forsake us.

One of my favorite songs was sung at Bryant's funeral: "His Eye Is on the Sparrow." Its words are still very true:

"Let not your heart be troubled," His tender word I hear,
And resting on His goodness, I lose my doubts and fears;
Though by the path He leadeth, but one step I may see;
His eye is on the sparrow, and I know He watches me;
His eye is on the sparrow, and I know He watches me.

Why should my heart be troubled, when all but hope is gone?
When Jesus is my fortress, my constant friend is He.
His eye is on the Sparrow, and I know He watches me.
His eye is on the Sparrow, and I know He watches me!"

Nothing can ever separate us from our Lord Jesus Christ: no death, nor life, nor darkness. He has promised to never leave us. I believe!

Reach Out and Touch

When our seventeen-year-old, Cathy, was a toddler, she contracted an ornery case of bronchitis. When the medication did not work at home she was hospitalized. They put her in an oxygen tent for controlled, vaporized breathing. I shall never forget the horrified look in her little eyes as she realized she was separated from us by that plastic enclosure. She could not understand.

She put her little hand to the plastic and we joined our palms to hers. There were tears on both sides. She, and we, felt cut-off and separated! The doctor came in and almost cried at the sight of our frustration. He suggested we take turns "unzipping" the tent and getting in with her. We did and everyone was happier.

There are occasions in life where we are "cut-off" from people. Various factors invade relationships that produce barriers which separate and inhibit growth. Sometimes we even choose to place barriers in order to protect or divide.

Through Jesus, God "unzips" the tent that humanity had erected and comes into our existence of fear, illness, and separation. He takes the initiative to reach out to us. If you find that you have erected a barrier between your heart and God's open arms, this is an excellent opportunity to tear down the barrier. Perhaps this is a great time to examine barriers for removal!

We have access to the loving Father! This access is not so much because we reach out to Him, but that we open "our tent" and let Him touch us. This access is what separates Christianity from other world religions! There are many ways to God but Jesus is the only way to the Loving Father!

Real Gift Giving

Watching a recent sunset, I thought of my dear friends and Christian family in Fiji, South Pacific. In the hurried, harried pace of living I recall their "laid-back" lifestyle. I hope to return there someday.

I recall a lesson they taught me about gift-giving. Before the U. S. missioners went from the hotel in Suva out into the "bush country", we procured extra towels for our two week, primitive mission. The mission was exhilarating. I stayed with Talatala (Rev.) Ciri's family. I had bought a special memento in the U. S. to give them as an expression of gratitude. I gave it to them the day before departure and they seemed formally appreciative.

I had come to realize their <u>need</u> for new towels, so I gave them the extras. They were ecstatically jubilant.

I carefully asked them why they were so responsive to the "used" towels instead of the "new" gift. They informed me that in Fiji, one doesn't give others "new" things that they, themselves, haven't used. The logic is that we should not give someone something that we haven't used and valued. They would not think of giving someone a <u>new</u> shirt that they had not worn and enjoyed!

As you consider gift-giving, what is the object of value that best symbolizes your affection? God gave the very best; therefore what <u>really</u> is our best to give?

Relaxed Power

Our daughter, Cathy, was once invited to Greenville for the Freedom Weekend Aloft hot air balloon fest. Her host family sponsored a balloon so she got to be a crew member for all the flights. She even got to fly once!

When we went to pick her up we were caught up in "joining the crew."

The professional pilot, Marc Van Dis from Grand Rapids, Michigan, moved with confidence as he gave order for "launch." I asked him what the key to flying a balloon was. He responded, "It is so very quiet up there. You have a sense of relaxed power!"

What an interesting juxtaposition: "relaxed power." It occurred to me that the phrase "relaxed power" also describes the Christian life. We have the promise that God will never cease to love us. We have the promise of Jesus that "I will be with you always." We do not face life alone but with a sense of "relaxed power" of God's presence.

This doesn't mean we are to <u>soar</u> above the problems and perplexities of life but rather we can face them with confidence, courage, and hope.

When the Hebrew people faced the Red Sea, they could not go around it, over it, or under it. They could only go through it. Moses held up his "rod" and reminded the people of the presence of God. A way was made.

My friends, these are great days! God is with us and we are with Him! Let us continue to explore our ministry together in the "relaxed power" of being yoked with God for His purpose and mission!

The Risk of Between

Recently I traveled to Atlanta, Georgia. For several years I have been invited to Emory University as a guest lecturer in the National Institute in Church Finance and Administration. It is a real joy to share with dedicated United Methodist leaders from around the country.

After passing through Athens, Georgia, I drove through a small community named "Between." That's right..."Between, Georgia." I don't think it is large enough for a zip code. I expected a city the size of Atlanta because I know a lot of people who live in "Between!" I know many who are reluctant to live either here or there so they live between.

Between laziness and hard work - (Don't want to be called an opportunist, so don't overdo it!)

Between aloofness and friendliness - (Don't want people to think I'm a snob but I wish to be left alone.)

Between withdrawal and commitment - (I just want to go to church and go home. Don't ask me to teach, serve or tithe.)

Between joy and despair - (I'll smile but I know something bad is about to happen to me so I'll not get too happy.)

Between Heaven and Hell - (I think I'm a Christian but I don't want to be a fanatic. I won't have any friends.)

"Between" is a difficult place to live! Living in "Between" breeds discontent. With a foot planted in two places one can risk serious neck injury.

I have heard that if you have one foot in ice and one foot in fire...on the average you are pretty good.

Our Lord invites you to move from "Between" to make some definite decisions about following Him. "Seek ye first the Kingdom of God and all these things will be added unto you."

"Do not put your hand to the plow and look back." "Take up your cross and follow me."

Perhaps this is the day that you decide to move from "Between" and to focus your vision upon the footsteps of Christ.

"Roger...Throttle Up"

Where were you when President John F. Kennedy was shot? Each of us (old enough) can tell exactly where we were and how that news impacted us. How about the spacecraft "Challenger"?

"Challenger" took off on a routine, though delayed, mission. The tragedy in the bright blue sky similarly impacted us then and the memory still hurts our hearts.

We momentarily salute folk heroes and winners of Super Bowls. When people give their lives in pursuit of their dream, they burn their identity into our memory. The Challenger crew dared to risk. S. C. native Ronald McNair, a brilliant physics scholar, had excelled at everything he attempted from playing a saxophone, to karate, to lab experiments on a previous shuttle flight.

Christa McAuliffe, the "teacher" in space, shared her joyful sense of discovery with her nation. She was "one of us," not a scientist or a PhD in anything. She was a smiling dreamer who dared to reach out to touch what she had not yet experienced: thus the essence of education.

The last heard words were Mike Smith's "Roger...Throttle Up!" Those words were symbolic of these adventurers' quest for the unknown.

Let us still thank God for their lives. May we in a childlike faith seek to express our Christian life and commitment in a fashion similar to the quest of these "Challengers". With our hand in God's hand, let us remember that Jesus has promised to be with us always! Then may we smile at the unknown and heroically proclaim, "Roger...Throttle Up!"

Slow Down And Enjoy The Trip.

Many folks today have been robbed of their trip through childhood. They are rushed along at too fast a pace. Little girls no longer have a raggedy Ann doll to squeeze but instead a Barbie doll with a face and figure that their mothers envy.

So these lives rush into marriage, and they have missed one of the best times of life. It is a free-wheeling time when a girl can spend all afternoon deciding what to wear to the party or a summer pondering whether she should become a nurse.

Those days seem to be gone when a boy will take a trip to the neighboring town on a bike or settle down to a comparative study of blondes as opposed to red-heads, without feeling that he has to make up his mind right away. Youth is a great time to live...and a terrible time to get married.

Yet adults have structured a world of growing up so fast that the young people do not have a chance to enjoy the trip. Thus, married too soon they switch from playing house to playing divorce.

Most of us have the impression that we must rush to where we are going. We are seen and heard racing along without pausing to savor the present and always looking ahead to some future time. This style of living rubs off into the realm of faith.

God wants us to enjoy the <u>journey</u> with him. He doesn't want us to just hurry along and think of nothing but heaven. God desires for us to experience the beauty of His creation today...to stop a moment and commune with Him. Jesus did not say, "At the end of the way you will find me." No, Jesus said, "I am the way..."

So don't wait to find God, or joy, or happiness at the <u>end</u> of the journey. Happiness and real joy is not the destination but the journey. Find them on the journey. This is where they are. Slow down and enjoy the trip.

The Sign Has Not Changed

I was watching the last World Series. Joe Garigiola was the announcer. There was a runner on first base. As the pitcher wound up, Joe said, "It's a pitchout." Sure enough it was a pitchout. Vin Scully was amazed and wondered how he could call the pitch. He said it was simple - the Mets were using the same signs that he had used as a catcher 25 years ago!

The catcher shows "signs" to the pitcher for a curve, fastball, change-up, pitchout, etc.

The signs for a vibrant church are the same today as they have been in the past. One sign is that we are seeing people come to faith in Jesus Christ. The last command of Jesus was to go into the world and share the Good News. The last command of Jesus should be the first concern of the church today! That sign hasn't changed at all.

Another sign is that people obey God's word through tithing. Jesus spoke more about money than He did any other single subject. The first tenth of all that comes to us is to be returned to His storehouse.

Another sign of a vibrant church is that the people love each other. Jesus said, "By this you shall know they are my disciples if they have love for one another." Churches that lavishly and liberally distribute their love find that love is always splendidly replenished.

Are these signs evident in your life? Do you tithe each month? Have you helped someone come to Jesus Christ and the church recently? Are you building bridges instead of walls? The signs are still the same. The application of those signs produce winners. Look at the World Series!

Smiling Nemani of Fiji

In 1980 I was invited by the World Methodist Council to join with twenty-five other Americans to go to the Fiji Islands not far from Australia and New Zealand. There I would meet one of my heroes of the faith, Dr. Alan Walker. The World Methodist Council was launching its 1980 decade of programs called "Mission to the 80's." They chose Fiji because 90% of Fijians are Christian and 90% of those Christians are Methodist. Fiji is the most Methodist country in the world.

We had a parade to the stadium where Dr. Alan Walker preached. When we arrived there were 40,000 Fijians ready to sing and celebrate and hear the great gospel proclaimed by Dr. Alan Walker. It's a moment I shall never forget.

On the following Tuesday we all divided to go to the "Bush Countries" where we would teach, preach and visit with native Fijians. Now you have to realize we were all a little concerned about the "Bush Country" because 150 years before we were there the Fijian Islands consisted of nothing but cannibals. Here we were five generations later being the only Caucasians in the villages with the Fijians who looked like Hawaiian people. I went in the full faith of God knowing that I would be safe.

One day we were traveling to another village in a jeep. I developed a great friendship there with a police inspector whose name is Aisake Rabuku. He was escorting me and the minister of that area, they call their preachers "Talatala". The Talatala and I were being driven by Aishke out to a new village.

We passed a young man who was on the side of the road. He waived and smiled very whimsically. They told me that his name was Nemani and what a wonderful young man he is in the local Church.

The village we went to was some miles away from where we saw Nemani. That evening we sat down for a wonderful dinner, Fijian style. That means we sat on the floor, a linen table cloth on the floor and we ate from bowls that had everything in gravy. The food was quite good.

While we were laughing and enjoying our meal someone came to the door and proclaimed "a runner is coming!" In Fiji they don't have telephones or TV's or electricity. They all live communally and help each other. They don't have jobs; they live as families in community. A runner meant that he was coming to bear news.

The runner came running into the hut where we were and shouted two words, "Nemani's dead, Nemani's dead." I found out the next morning what had happened. Nemani's father had gone on a hunting expedition and left chores for Nemani to complete around the house. Upon returning from the hunting trip, he discovered all the chores had not been completed. He grew angry with Nemani and beat him with his hand. The first time ever in Nemani's life, the first time the father had done that; he lost his temper. Nemani could not handle his father's rejection. He hung himself in the tree behind their hut and had been found dead.

The next day I was sitting with the Talatala who said to me, "Ernie, I've never in my ministry been asked to conduct a funeral for someone who has committed suicide. I do not know what to say. I'm afraid that I will say the wrong thing. Since you're leaving our country in a few days, would you please head the remarks at Nemani's funeral service?"

With fear and trepidation I said "With God's help, yes, I will do it." From that point forward I began to mull in my heart what would be the right word. If I said the wrong thing I would encourage other young people to commit suicide. If I said the wrong thing then I would cause even worse guilt and anguish upon his father. With great prayer, I approached that moment.

The Fijians, as I said, live a simple life. They try to live just like the people did in the New Testament days. At the time of the funeral they had erected this large open air hut outside of Nemani's house. Three hundred Fijians came and sat under the hut. Just like at Church the men were on the left, the women on the right, and a 75 voice choir sat across the front where they sang beautiful hymns accapella.

It came time for; me to bring my remarks. I stepped up to the table where I was to kneel, I did so. I noticed some noises. The first one is like in the

New Testament when their prodigal son came home, there were some people beside the hut butchering a calf. And then I heard some women inside the hut wailing as they did in the New Testament. I whispered to the Talatala, "Please ask the wailers to come join us." Thank goodness they stopped their wailing and came to worship. I then said a few words to the crowd and read to them from Romans Chapter 8.

> *"What then shall we say to these things? If God is for us, who can be against us? He who did not spare his own Son but gave him up for us all, how will he not also with him graciously give us all things? Who shall bring any charge against God's people? It is God who justifies. Who is to condemn? Christ Jesus is the one who died—more than that, who was raised—who is at the right hand of God, who indeed is interceding for us. Who shall separate us from the love of Christ? Shall tribulation, or distress, or persecution, or famine, or nakedness, or danger, or sword? As it is written,*
>
> *"For your sake we are being killed all the day long; we are regarded as sheep to be slaughtered."*
>
> *No, in all these things we are more than conquerors through him who loved us. For I am sure that neither death nor life, nor angels nor rulers, nor things present nor things to come, nor powers, nor height nor depth, nor anything else in all creation, will be able to separate us from the love of God in Christ Jesus our Lord.*

Once I had finished I looked at the crowd and then looked the father in the eye and said what I truly believe in my heart because of these words in Romans 8. When Nemani's spirit left his body he stepped into the loving arms of our heavenly father, who said to him, "Nemani, Nemani, what have you done? What have you done?" And he put his arms around Nemani and took him to Heaven. As the scripture says, nothing can separate us from the love of God found in Jesus Christ our Lord.

Following the funeral we walked as a parade down the dirt road. We took a left on another dirt road, and probably walked a mile to the burial site of Nemani. Nemani's body was in a press board casket with a glass window. Looking in you could tell that Nemani had hung himself; you could see the rope marks on his neck. The pallbearers carried the body in the casket the entire length.

We got to the grave site. In Fiji the Fijian women will spend months and months working on this beautiful mat that goes on the floors of their huts. It's made of dried pineapple leaves and then dyed in different colors, blacks, and reds. It may take six women five months to make one mat. When we got to Nemani's grave, they had put two poles across this big hole in the ground and all the families who had come had brought a mat. There were probably 30 mats stacked up on those poles, upon which they put Nemani's casket. After a scripture and a prayer the pallbearers pulled out the two poles and the casket sank with those mats down into a humongous hole. They then took the mats and wrapped up around the casket. Hours and hours of love by the Fijian women were symbolized by those mats wrapping around Nemani's body.

His mother had a pillow that she had embroidered Nemani's name on that was placed under the head of the casket. Those were made for the Fijian children when they are born. And then the family gathered around this massive hole in the ground and they began to push the dirt in to bury Nemani. After a few minutes other Church members gathered with them to help and in a matter of thirty minutes the hole had been covered with fresh dirt and mounded up about six feet high above the ground.

That is death in Fiji. The good news that I shared with them is still true today. Nothing can separate us from the love of God and Christ Jesus our Lord. In memory of Nemani let us claim this truth for our hearts and our families.

Staying In the Game

Another story comes to mind when I was a young boy. My Daddy, Cecil Nivens, coached the little league baseball team. My older brother, Jimmy was a star at baseball and I wanted to be a star like my brother but I didn't have his skills. I was just a little asthmatic kid.

I tried out for my Daddy's little league team one year, there was one extra player more than he could have on the team. So he had another fellow and I draw straws, and I was lucky enough to draw the right straw and got to pay on my daddy's team. It was the highlight of my childhood. I didn't play all year because I wasn't very good. At the end of the year we were playing our last game.

We were playing it under the lights of night and all the parents and friends had come to watch us play. It was quite a setting. Our team toward the end of the game was losing and so I figured my Daddy had nothing to lose if he let me bat. When I was going to bat there were two runners on base and several of the team players came to me and said "Ernie, Ernie, listen, if you make an out the game is over so be careful up there." One of them said, "Let me tell you what to do; if you tip the catcher's mitt they'll call interference on the catcher and you'll go to first base; it's just like you got a hit. So if you can tip his mitt with your bat they'll call interference and the game will continue." I said "Okay I'll do it." He said "But wait until you get two strikes, don't make is so obvious." I said "Okay will do." So sure enough I got up there and there came two balls because I was so small. Then came the first strike and then a third ball and then another strike. It was a loaded count, three balls and two strikes.

I knew my time had come. When the pitcher wound up and threw the ball, I turned a little bit and slammed my bat down on the catcher's mitt. Oh it was such a mistake! The catcher rolled around the ground crying, screaming, and holding his hand. They told me later that they thought I had broken his hand. The umpire called interference on the catcher and I went to first base and then later I scored a run when somebody hit a ball so far that it cleared the bases. I felt like a hero for a little while.

The game continued because we had tied the score. So daddy told me to go in and play second base. I never played second base before. I was out there hoping the ball didn't come to me. Eventually someone hit it and they just hit it over my head. I was relieved it was going to go over my head into right field but just in case I jumped up with my glove as high as I could then I turned to run into right field to chase the ball. After about four steps I noticed I couldn't find the ball. I asked the right fielder, I said "Where's the ball?" He said "Ernie, look in your glove!" And sure enough I looked in my glove and I had caught the ball, I didn't even know it. It was the third out.

As I came running back to the dugout all the fans on our side were giving me a standing ovation for catching that ball. I shall never forget that feeling of being the hero of that moment. How much my daddy did for me by taking a chance on me and a risk on me, hoping that I could do the right thing. Well swinging the bat I did the wrong thing but playing second base I finally did something right.

Isn't that the way God is with us? Sometimes we mess up but God doesn't give up on us. He keeps us "in the game." That's the way it is with our lives. God never gives up on us. God never fails us. He's always with us, he promised never to leave us. That's the way it is when you're a child of God.

Sharing A Magic Potion

There was a nice story in a recent issue of the newspaper. A policeman, distraught over daily facing crime, death and despair, has volunteered to serve his local hospital. He did not volunteer to help with security or to work in the emergency room. He goes to the newborn nursery, scrubs, dresses, sits in a rocking chair and <u>hugs</u> newborn babies.

Many studies indicate newborns who are cuddled and caressed are healthier than those who are neglected. That fact remains true as we continue to grow. Obviously this policeman has found a "magic potion" to provide balance in his life. The quietness and tenderness he receives from these babies help him face a dark and cruel world.

When our daughter Emily was small she would often crawl into my lap and say "Daddy, I'm hug hungry!" We would sit quietly and just hug.

Our world needs a lot more huggers. Most of us respond more quickly to encouragement and affirmation than we do put-downs and intimidation. I understand the Church to be a place where people affirm, encourage, and support each other--hugging. People who experience hugs usually don't experiment with drugs.

Are you hug hungry? The very best way to get a hug is to give one. "God so loved the world that He sent His only Son..." to hold out his arms and <u>hug</u> us into His love.

Shoot For The Moon: Think Big—Dream Big Work Big

My Daddy said, "Shoot for the moon. You may hit the street light, but at least you got off the ground."

Once I attended the Million Dollar Round Table (MDRT) meeting in New Orleans. MDRT is the top 3% of life insurance agents in the world. Each morning we have 3 ½ hours of various speakers: motivational, inspirational and educational. Sometimes it is someone famous like Christopher Reeves and Charlton Heston; sometimes it is someone we haven't heard of before who touches our hearts.

This day John Beltzer of New York City told his story. In the mid 1980's, his fraternal twin committed suicide, leaving him with a struggle of grief and depression. His brother was a talented musician and songwriter. John had hopes that they would reach stardom. Without his brother his life became somewhat aimless.

Walking down the street one day, he envisioned how he should spend his life. He made a heart decision to write songs for children with terminal illness and chronic disease. The songs he would write would include particular facts about each child's life: their pet, hobbies, grandparent's names, brothers, sisters, favorite song, etc.

He told us several stories of how these individualized songs would help the children survive moments of pain and emotional anguish.

He asked for our help. He had just completed a song for Alyson and felt that the chorus needed a large choir. He realized what better choir than the 7,000 voices of MDRT. After teaching us the chorus, we then turned the New Orleans Convention Center into a giant recording studio. With tears in our eyes, hearts filled with joy, we sang a song for little Alyson. John was given a ten minute standing ovation.

The next day he came back to the stage and played for us a video showing Alyson hearing us sing her song for the very first time. My words here cannot begin to express the emotion of mine and 7,000 other hearts. Alyson was brought on stage and courageously looked out at the 7,000 faces and said, "Thank you, MDRT, for my song." The MDRT Foundation awarded John a $50,000 grant. (For more information, go to www.songsoflove.org)

This is a fantastic story of how a young man turned one of the darkest moments of his life into bright white hope for struggling children. His story and the choices that he has made comfort me with questions about how I should use disappointments in my life as a catalyst for loving service to others. I come away from MDRT with a renewed commitment of finding ways to touch people with hope.

Now it is your turn – you may be carrying a basketful of grief, worry and anxiety. John Beltzer's story challenges us to find a way to channel that negative energy into positive life flow.

"Shoot for the moon; think big, dream big, work big"

This goes back to my daddy, Cecil J. Nivens, who died at 50 years old. I was 27 when he passed away. He had such an impact on me and still does. I included this before but I'll repeat it here. He said, "Ernie, shoot for the moon. If you hit the street light, at least you got off the ground." My daddy patterned for me the art of thinking big. Now, I grew up on a mill hill in Rock Hill, South Carolina and had a lot to transcend in growing up.

In my elementary school, out of 12 who graduated 8th grade, I think ten of us either are dead or went to jail. It was a tough neighborhood. By my daddy taught me how to transcend, to think beyond that. It's easy to get mired into micro living the details of every day, but we've got to have a dream.

When it comes to my dreams, I could give you a long list. My dreams are centered around my family. Rosemarie, my wife, and I have three wonderful daughters Cathy, Noelle, and Emily; three sons-in-law, Kevin, Bo and Jon; five grandchildren Eric, Matthew, Kristin, Justin and Ryan.. My dream is just to have them around as much as possible. My dream is to do special things for them.

The money that I make has no value. It's the value we attach to the money. One of my favorite things to do with the family is to take a summer vacation each year. We rent a house on Pawley's Island, South Carolina for a week and everyone comes. I've focused on my grandchildren more and more. I love to read or tell them bedtime stories and rock them to sleep.

You know, life doesn't get any better than sitting on the front porch in a rocking chair with the ocean breezes coming around you, looking at the stars and moon and holding my grandchildren. You look in their eyes and see the parade of their ancestors going by and the canvas that they will paint their lives on. Is there anything higher than that in life? I don't think so. Yeah, I want to travel a lot. It's not the material things that excite me. It's grandchildren's eyes that keep me working hard.

That's what keeps me shooting for the moon physically and spiritually.

Some of Our Favorite Little Things

When Mark Twain's daughter, Susy, was very small, she once cried because a picnic had been canceled due to rain.

While trying to console herself she had broken a favorite toy. Her mother tried to comfort her, saying, "There, there, Susy. You mustn't cry over little things." The child's reply, although ungrammatical, was profoundly philosophical: "Mamma, what is little things?"

During December we prepare for Christmas. The shops and television would have us "buy into" the value system that bigger is better, and even bigger is even better. We are tempted to demonstrate the quality of our love and affection with the quantity and size of the gift. That is ridiculous, isn't it!?

What enormous thing can you buy that would completely symbolize your love for your spouse, child, parent, neighbor, etc.? It is the little things that go to make up Christmas. Christmas began in a little manger, with a little baby, in a little town, in a little country.

The joy of Christmas is not in the size of the box but the celebration of the big things of life wrapped in little packages. When it comes, have a very Merry Little Christmas!!

Surprise!!

Life is full of surprises! Rosemarie left home recently to go to church. She stopped for the light and then turned right. Suddenly, a Highway Trooper she had noticed at the intersection came quickly behind her with blue light flashing.

After pulling over, he asked the usual questions concerning license and registration. He then asked her place of employment and she became curious. She asked, "Would you tell me what I did wrong?"

He replied, "Oh, ma'am. You didn't do anything wrong. It's Memorial Day weekend and we're rewarding good driving!" He then told her all the things she had done right: seat belt, proper lane change, etc. He handed her a folder of goodies: a map, litter bag, a "Junior Trooper" Badge, and more. To say the least, she was surprised!

Life is full of surprises! Easter morning was the greatest surprise in history. Jesus, who was dead on Friday resurrected and reappeared. Mary and his disciples were overwhelmed. One of them, Thomas of course, refused to believe it until he saw him. When he did he got a big surprise.

The Risen Christ has surprised people throughout history. He surprises believers with hope, joy, open doors, opportunities, strength and grace. The list of surprises is a long one

If you have trouble believing this, then just try believing and following Jesus and you will, also, have a big surprise. God is good and life is full of surprises.

The Talking Church

The other day I rode in one of those new cars that talk to you. Yes, in a deep male computerized voice with excellent manners, it spoke English. Upon getting in it said, "Please fasten your seat belt." The door didn't quite close, so patiently it reprimanded, "The door is ajar!"

Then riding down the road it suddenly broke in upon the silence with "Your fuel is low!" Now to tell you the truth I realize that we Americans have had a love affair with our autos but this is perhaps going too far.

I began to wonder what it would be like if other things were to talk to us. Then I surmised, "How would it be if our churches could talk to us?" Yes, can't you see it? You walk into the vestibule and the church says, "Please take a pew toward the front!"

Each pew would be equipped with a little speaker. Varying admonitions would be forthcoming:

"Please do not whisper during the prayer!"

"Please put a larger amount in the offering plate before you pass it!"

"Do not snore during the sermon!"

Are there any investors ready to back this new concept in spiritual instruction?

Well, of course, this notion is a bit far-fetched, especially when we realize that we already have a "still small voice" that speaks to us in worship.

As we prepare to come to worship we will hear God's voice. It may come in the prayer, the choir's beautiful anthem, the singing of our marvelous hymns, in the Scripture lesson, or in the preached Word.

Let's concentrate this Sunday upon hearing scriptural voices: angels, shepherds, a loving Mother, a caring Father, or adoring Nazarenes and Bethlehemites, prodigal sons, lost sheep, and etcetera. If we truly listen then we will hear. "Those that have ears let them hear..."

A Thankful Thanksgiving

Each year as we approach Thanksgiving I am compelled to yield to a time of memory. I enjoy quietly sitting to re-live some great days at my Grandmother's home with my Daddy's side of the family. Yet one particular Thanksgiving emerges.

For several years Daddy drove a Murray Cookie Truck in the Rock Hill-York-Gastonia route. I often enjoyed riding the route all day with him in exchange for a free "giant" Baby Ruth candy bar.

I would pretend sickness so I could lay out of school and work with him. One year he was told he had to work on Thanksgiving Day. I really felt sorry for him and volunteered to help.

We went to Grandmother's about 5:00 am. She had packed sack lunches for us. After running from country store to grocery store all morning we ended up at noon outside Blacksburg, SC.

Daddy drove the truck off a side road up a very high hill. We settled under some oaks on Mt. Croghan overlooking a beautiful expanse toward Greenville and the Blue Ridge Mountains.

In our sacks were turkey sandwiches, deviled eggs, etc. We didn't talk much. The squirrels danced to the tune of rustling oak leaves. High white clouds were like angel's hands praising Creation from their royal background. Our silence was heavy with the love of father and son.

Sometimes I walk in the woods. The crunching leaves and scampering squirrels help me to be a twelve-year-old once more. I feel Daddy's closeness and thank God.

"Now Thank We All Our God..."

To The Least of Them

We all despise those experiences where we feel we are "wasting our time". We want our time and energy to "add up" to something significant. We avoid investing ourselves in <u>vain</u>.

Sometimes we take a risk to care and find out that, apparently, our care is in vain. Early in my ministry, I was a student pastor to several rural churches. I met one evening with other church people in the "downtown" church. Our meeting was interrupted by some transients seeking "gas money".

As I listened, the downtown preacher turned them away. When I asked why, he replied, "They were just bums looking for some beer money." I grew angry, remembering Jesus' words, "When you have done it unto the least of these, you have done it unto me."

I caught them before they drove away and gave them $5 of my $6. At the time dollars didn't come easy! The downtown preacher said, "You are a fool! They will go to the first juke-joint and drink up your money." I agreed that they just might. I couldn't control how they used my gift, but I knew I did the right thing by responding.

On my way home I drove past a "juke-joint" and, sure enough, their car was there. They were "drinking up" my five dollars. I never told that to the downtown preacher! I just prayed that someone else might reach them with love.

I don't know what became of them. We do what we can in Jesus' name and trust Him for the correct response. Sure we should be wise in our giving, but we should not let false-wisdom be our excuse for not responding.

All this came back to me when I heard Rev. Will Rogers (who is now in the heavenly choir), preach from 1 Corinthians 15:58, "Therefore be steadfast, immovable, always abounding in the work of the Lord, knowing that in the Lord your labor is not in vain."

Let us continue to work in Jesus' name and our work will not be in vain! We will be Evangels of Care.

A Tribute to a Mother

A poor widow's son down in Texas, struck it rich with oil, and as Mother's Day approached, made up his mind to show his appreciation by some unusual gift for all mother had done for him. So he told the owner of a pet shop: "What is your most unusual and expensive pet?"

The Merchant answered: "I have a Mynah bird worth $27,000. It is the only one in the world that can recite the Lord's Prayer, the 23rd Psalm and the 13th chapter of First Corinthians."

"I'll take it," said the Texan. "I don't care how much it costs. Mom is worth it, and she will get so much comfort hearing it recite Scripture."

So he bought it and shipped it off to his mother.

On Monday following Mother's Day, he called her long distance. "Did you get my bird?" he asked.

"Yes, son."

"How did you like it?"

"It was delicious, son."

That's so sadly funny it hurts, doesn't it? In our convenient age it is so easy to "ship off" a present to our mothers. The best gift to mother is not so much a thing but a gift of self.

If you have your mother with you, give her your time...

a time to honor,

a time to encourage,

a time to support,

a time to console,

a time to pray,

a time to remember,

a time to appreciate,

a time to forgive,

a time to be forgiven.

If you do not have your mother, find a "stand in" mother and love her. You'll both be happier and fulfilled.

What's In Your TV??

Recent research says that when the average American teenager turns 18, they have seen 22,000 hours of TV programming and 600,000 commercials totaling some 3 years of their life. And what has been seen in those accumulative 3 years?--Thousands of murders, beatings, fights, rapes, shootings and clubbings.

One little boy, whose TV broke, thought the TV repairman had come to clean out all the dead cowboys and soldiers.

There seems to be a glorification of the sicknesses of society. We have become a society without a moral center, like a doughnut: good things around the edges but no guidelines. People today seem to be caught up in a spirit of discouragement in a tide of purposelessness and materialism that threatens our society with decay and destruction.

Routinely in communities around the country young people are shocked by the several accidents and deaths among their school mates. Suddenly the reality of trauma and death moves from the TV and movie screens into their reality with pain and confusion. I sense our young people groping for answers and hope!

The answer is a positive faith. A positive faith in a loving and caring heavenly Father can make a new difference and get us going in a new way.

Young people: the presence of the living, risen Jesus Christ will walk by your side to give you hope, courage, and meaningless. God has a plan for life that will bring you joy and fulfillment.

He will reach through you to others--giving them hope and courage as well. Consider Christ!

When You Wish

Jiminy Cricket said to Pinocchio: "When you wish upon a star, makes no difference who you are!" Wouldn't it be wonderful if we could always keep those child-like qualities? It's so easy for a child to expect the whole world to be beautiful.

When I was a young boy I liked to lay out on warm nights upon the stoop by the front steps of our mill hill house: 114 Long Street, Rock Hill, SC. I would gaze at the immensity of the universe and wonder. On clear nights (and when the street light was burned out) I could see stars beyond the regular visible ones. I thought often about Jiminy Cricket's promise.

The danger is that as we mature, we become more cynical and lose our capacity to wish upon a star and to dream our dreams. We become too interested in facts that we lose the romance and the mystery of life.

God has given us the capacity to be a child with the ability to wish, to wonder, and to dream.

I'm always meeting people who have a vibrant faith--they are childlike. Jesus said: "Except you become as a little child, you shall not enter the Kingdom of God." (Matthew 18:3) When I meet someone who has experienced Jesus Christ, I have met a person who is childlike! Being childlike in Christ you'll dare to dream. You'll dream impossible dreams, because when God gives you a dream it's always an impossible dream (for us alone but not with Him).

God wants us to wish upon the Star--He has made us with that potential! He wants us to dream! What is your dream?

What Seagulls Teach Us

One week our whole family was able to take a mini-retreat to the beach. (That's not an easy feat with our multi-scheduled lives.) We laughed, slept late, ate well, and celebrated a joyful peace. It's our favorite time to walk on the beach!

One of the joys is to feed the seagulls. Emily is afraid of anything that doesn't speak English, so I had to coach her a bit. I told her that the gulls are at first afraid of humans but after a few minutes they will eat from your hand. Sure enough, after the first few pieces of bread and popcorn they flew face-to-beak and delicately extracted the food from our fingers. It was exciting!

Afterwards we talked about how they came to trust and depend on us. It is much like our relationship with God. In our blessed style of living in America, we are always in need of God.

We don't always sense that need. In impoverished areas of America and the world the people's dependency upon God is more evident. In America we have to discipline ourselves to focus upon our dependence.

Much of the Bible depicts various individuals as they struggle with their dependency upon God. From Adam and Eve to the rich farmer Jesus called a "fool", we see God calling people to a deeper dependence. God doesn't want "burnt offerings and sacrifices" so much as a dependent "walk in the garden."

As we prepare our hearts for the new day each and every day, let us discipline ourselves to focus upon God's presence and <u>depend</u> upon His love and guidance.

You May Have Already Won

*E*d McMahon gets on my nerves! He teases. With his deeply authoritative voice he proclaims. "You <u>may have</u> already won ten million dollars!" You can take all his "may haves" and one dollar and by a Coke.

A Hispanic man who speaks little English walked into a pharmacy in Brooklyn seeking to cash his lottery ticket for $24. When the clerk checked it, the discovery was made that the man's ticket was worth 1.6 million dollars. When the clerk tried to explain that to the Hispanic man, the man got very upset and stalked angrily out of the store.

Some people pursued him and finally communicated to him what had happened. He was one of three persons who would split 4.8 million. The man had a ticket worth $79,000 for the next 20 years, but he almost did not understand.

As Christians we <u>have</u> something to share that is more important than 1.6 million dollars. Money can be unwisely spent or stolen, but the LIFE that Jesus Christ brings is something that no one can take away, and no money can buy.

That life is available to every person, yet so many people walk around in this world without realizing that God has offered it to them. It's not that we "may have" qualified for it but that we <u>have</u> it available to us!

Oftentimes the problem is communication. People who have received the life that Jesus Christ came to bring sometimes fail to communicate that to other people. Some folk just go to Church and settle for a $24 religion when they could <u>have</u> a multi-trillion dollar faith!

Some stay angrily frustrated because they don't understand all that God wants to give.

The greatest gift in the world is available to us--if we claim it. We are already winners of the greatest prize possible. Claim it---share it!

Your Silence Is So Loud

About a decade ago I was invited to come to an office in Texas to make an hour's presentation on the skill of reading personality styles. I love doing those kinds of workshops and entered it with a great deal of excitement. I made a presentation with vigor and passion and convincingly showed the participants how to effectively read people and help them make decisions. There were about 200 people in the audience. Forty-five minutes into my presentation, one man stood up and interrupted me.

"I don't believe this hogwash. There is no way that you can read people's personalities the way you're describing. People are too complex to be able to boil down in a few minutes. You can't possibly know who they are and how they think and what their desires are."

People were kind of looking embarrassed and shifting away from him. They were ashamed that he had interrupted a guest in their midst.

I paused a second and replied, "You and I have never met, have we?

"No, we haven't."

"May I ask you a question?"

He looked daggers at me, but he finally said, "Sure."

"I have just one question for you. How does your wife enjoy driving her green minivan?"

He sat down. I had him. Everyone broke into laughter and applauded the fact that I had quieted him. I went on to finish my workshop to the great delight of those attending. A lot of questions followed.

After the workshop the loud man marched straight up to me and demanded, "Tell me how you did that. How did you know my wife drives a green minivan?"

"Sorry," I replied, I don't speak with people who so rudely interrupt me. You'll have to excuse me."

Now that was abnormal behavior for me, but I was serious. We saw each other a year later, and he again marched up to me and wanted to know how I did it. I still refused to answer him. It was another year before we saw each other again. He demanded once again with less in his voice. I told him I wasn't ready to tell him yet, but if he was nice, I might tell him one day.

The next year, now three years after the original event, he said, "Ernie, I'm sorry about what I did that day; it's really been bothering me. I would really like to know how you were able to tell me what you did about my wife's car by just looking at me."

"I said, "Well, when you were dressing me down, I noticed that you were wearing a wedding ring. I was able to determine that the only person who would stand up in a group of his peers and take on a popular speaker was off the chart high-driver personality. It's the same kind of person who says that if this doesn't work, give me a bigger hammer and I'll fix it. From that I determined you were one of those people."

"Okay, all right, I admit that. You had me, but how did you know about my wife's car?"

"Well, in studying personality styles I learned there is a compatibility chart indicating the kind of person who would marry someone with your personality. The only woman who would marry you had to be an off the chart amiable. Someone of that personality type likes to keep her world even and doesn't rock the boat. When she gets a car, she likes to have one that holds several passengers like a station wagon or the now popular minivan. That was an informed guess on my part. An amiable's favorite colors are usually blue or green. I guessed that her car was green and at that point I was just plain lucky. The color was a 50/50 guess."

He just laughed, and every time we see each other since then, we laugh about his wife's car.

The point of the story is that there is great power that comes by studying how to determine personality styles. It is possible to determine both primary and secondary styles. Sometimes the person they show to us is not the person they are when they are around their family or best friend.

The challenge is to develop that skill. It's not a gift; it is a skill. There are a number of publications that can train us to do this. With that skill developed we can listen to people and let them tell us who they are. Once we know more about their who-ness, we can talk about their dreams, their hopes and solve their fears. Then we are more capable caring Christians.

We Are So Squeezable

Charmin toilet paper has used an ad on TV which has imprinted their product on Americans minds as being squeezably soft. Mr. Whipple, who is very shy, has to call a halt to all the shoppers who find Charmin so irresistible that they feel compelled to pick it up and squeeze it. In the end, Mr. Whipple, usually, with great embarrassment, finds himself guilty of squeezing the Charmin.

Well, Charmin is not the only thing that is squeezed. People are too, and not only in the embrace of affection. Paul, talking to the Christians in Rome says, "Do not be conformed to this world" (Rom. 12:2). The Phillip's translation says, "Do not let the world squeeze you into its own mold." And that type of squeezing is bad, for you lose your individuality as a Child of God and merely take the shape of the society which pressures you into its own mold.

Jesus Christ marched to the music of God. He was a non-conformist and did not compromise His principles with the standards of the world in His day. He calls us to march to His music of love, grace, forgiveness, and enabling people to reach their God-given potential. You will probably quite often be out of step with those around you, and some might even think you peculiar.

These are the days to do your own thing in responsible Christian love, and don't be squeezed like Charmin tissue.

We Could Not Do Without You

Have you ever had a feeling that you were of no account and never would be; that in spite of all God had done for you, you were a failure? There are few things more fraught with heartache and bitterness than that.

There are a lot of folk who come to that dismal conviction. They work and nobody seems to appreciate it. They toil and nobody compliments them.

Frank Boreham wrote an essay that spoke of a certain discouraged friend of his. He wished to help his friend by sending him a gift.

The strange present he was going to send was an onion. Yes, he was going to wrap this onion in lovely tissue paper and put it in a beautiful candy box tied with pink ribbon.

Now, why send him an onion? Well, though it is the most valuable of all vegetables, nobody praises the onion! You read great poems on daffodils, violets, roses, and daises. A great poet even wrote about a louse and a field mouse but where do you find a poem about an onion? What bride ever carries a bouquet of onions?

This is true, but why? Not because the onion is useless but because it is so strong.

It is hard to grow sentimental over great strong things though tears have been shed over onions. There are some we praise, you know, because we think that they need it to keep going.

They are weak and need boosting. There are others we do not praise because they are strong and we expect strong things of them.

So it is not wise to conclude that because nobody is praising you that you are of no account to the world. Like the onion we could not do without you!

We Have Not Been Left Alone!

I have a minister friend who had an interesting experience a few years ago. While in seminary he saved his money for golf lessons, searched out a "Pro" at a country club, and made an appointment. The Pro took him to the driving range, collected the $150 fee, gave a couple of tips and went to answer the phone. Forty-five minutes later the Pro had not returned.

The minister inquiringly walked to the club house to discover the Pro had resigned that morning and had just left town. My friend was left holding the bag and feeling like a triple bogey.

The disciples huddled behind locked doors of the Upper Room following the crucifixion. They felt afraid and abandoned. Into their fear came Jesus offering peace and hope. He did not just come promising "lessons" only to skip town with their hope. He returned to fulfill His word.

In the weeks after Easter we still feel in the "glow" of Easter. I use the word "glow" instead of "afterglow" because the "glow" of Easter is never over. We make the mistake of celebrating "anticipation" more than the event. We relish preparing for Christmas and look forward to Easter but the event is often anti-climactic leaving us feeling a little depressed or "let down".

For me the power of Easter is the reality that our Risen Lord continues to make His presence known, as He did with the disciples. He invades our darkness, challenges our fear, and joyfully overpowers our gloom.

We are called to be "Easter People" who continue His model of invading the dark places in our world, challenging fear by walking with The Shepherd, singing joyfully at funerals, and denouncing gloom with bubbling grace. Sure, we will falter but by faith we can "rise up" to victory because we are EASTER PEOPLE! We have not been left alone!

What Happens In Us

I heard some years ago about a man who worked in a railroad yard in Virginia. It is said that his particular job was to make sure at the end of the day that each refrigerated boxcar's doors were closed. Then no cold air from the refrigeration units would be wasted. At the end of one day, he was closing the doors.

One boxcar's door was jammed, and he could not get it closed. So he got up in the car and worked with the door until he freed the jam. The door slammed shut. Unfortunately he could not get out. He was locked in the boxcar all night long. His family worried when he didn't come home. His coworkers, thinking he had already left, went to their homes.

They found him the next morning in that boxcar. He was dead. This refrigerated car would normally have sustained a temperature of about 32 to 38 degrees, but its refrigeration unit was broken. The worker didn't know that.

They found him on the wooden floor of the car with messages scratched into the floor's wooden surface. The first message said, "I am freezing to death." "Tell my family I love them; I am dying," was the second message. And then, he died. The temperature that night never got colder than 53 degrees outside and 55 degrees inside the car. He thought he was freezing to death, and convinced of that fact in his mind, he froze to death.

Now here is the point of this story. What happens to us is not as important as what happens in us. In this mission as Evangels of Care, there are a number of challenges. Sometimes we are rejected. Sometimes we give a lot of time and concern trying to help someone only to have them shut it down with no results. That's the life of an Evangel.

Not everyone wants to hear the good news. We have to keep remembering that every event has some teaching measure to it. We have to remember what happened to this man in the Virginia railroad yard; his lesson applies. Indeed, what happens to us is not as important as what happens in us.

As Evangels of Care let us remember, **"I can do all things through Christ, who strengthens me."** Philippians 4:13.

When You Come To the Detour

Back in 1915 there was a deplorable condition in Coffee County, Alabama. In this heart of the cotton belt, the boll weevil viciously attacked the cotton crop and stripped away the livelihood of the people. They seemed stuck hopelessly in depression. However, some ears perked up to the counsel of scientist George Washington Carver, as he told people about the value of raising peanuts.

In the peanut he had found riches: chemicals for soap, ink, paper, plastics, shampoo, etc. The people responded and by 1919, with peanuts as the main crop, Coffee County was experiencing prosperity. The boll weevil which seemed like a curse became a blessing.

So in 1919 a monument was erected to the boll weevil with the following inscription: "In profound appreciation to the boll weevil, and what it has done as the herald of prosperity, this monument is erected by the citizens of Enterprise, Coffee County, Alabama."

I recently told this story in a speaking engagement. One of the listeners sent me a small statue of this monument. I cherish it and have it prominently displayed in my office.

As we walk with God we can accept life's changes without being bowled over by them. We need not fear change, but see it as an opportunity for growth and new discovery. When you come to the detour, don't curse the interruption but thank God for the new scenery you will see.

In the midst of life's transitions remember there is a love that never changes. It remains constant and true. It is found in Jesus Christ who is the same yesterday, today, and forever.

We can continue because He lives. I offer a tribute to Bill and Gloria Gaither who wrote the blessed song that has blessed my life and thousands of others.

Because He lives, I can face tomorrow,
Because I know He holds the future,
And life is worth the living,
Just because He lives!

ABOUT THE AUTHOR

C. Ernie Nivens hails from Rock Hill, South Carolina, where he graduated from Rock Hill High School. He entered the ministry with the United Methodist Church in 1970 while working his way through college. Nivens finished Francis Marion University, Florence, SC in 1976 with a BA is English. He then completed (along with his wife, Rosemarie) his M.Div (Masters of Divinity) from Candler School of Theology, Emory University, Atlanta Georgia in 1979 while serving a church on the weekend and working part time on a General Motors assembly line. He then served various appointments until 1989. During this time he served on two international church missions to the Fiji Islands and to Seoul, Korea and was a church consultant to many churches around the United States.

He retired from parish ministry in 1990 and began his career as a financial service professional. His hunger for education led him to complete his Masters of Science in Financial Services, MSFS, with the Accredited Estate Planner, AEP, in 2002. He has been a very popular speaker in hundreds of meetings within the industry. He has been associated the entire time with a major Mutual Life Insurance Company with over 10,000 agent/representatives. He has finished each year's production in the top 100 even the top 50 of 10,000+.

He has been married to Rosemarie for 41 years. They have three daughters, Cathy, Noelle, and Emily and three sons-in-law, Kevin, Bo and Jon. They are, also, very proud grandparents of five grandchildren, Eric, Matthew, Kristin, Justin and Ryan.

He is associated with Ed Slott, CPA from New York City as a Master Elite Ira Advisor. He serves on the Advisory Council for the Ed Slott Company, LLC (www.irahelp.com).

This book is the first of several yet to come.